ATHEISM

UNRAVELED

ATHEISM
UNRAVELED

Powerful Proofs for the Existence of God

MATTHEW CSERHATI

credo
house publishers

Atheism Unraveled

Copyright © 2016 by Matthew Cserhati

Published in the United States by Credo House Publishers,
a division of Credo Communications LLC, Grand Rapids, Michigan
www.credohousepublishers.com

ISBN: 978-1-625860-50-7

Cover design by Nicolas Mulder
Interior design by Nicolas Mulder
Editing by Donna Huisjen

Printed in the United States of America

First edition

To all of my brothers and sisters in the faith
as well as to all victims of Communism and abortion.

"The heavens declare the glory of God; and the firmament
sheweth his handywork."
(Psalm 19:1)

"The fool hath said in his heart, There is no God.
Corrupt are they, and have done abominable iniquity: there
is none that doeth good."
(Psalm 53:1)

Contents

Chapter 1: The nature of the debate **1**

Chapter 2: Science, knowledge, and skepticism **7**

Chapter 3: Proofs for God from creation **11**

Chapter 4: Theophanies and spiritual manifestations **29**

Chapter 5: Why is there suffering? **39**

Chapter 6: Communism: the first atheist state **45**

Chapter 7: Morality and the appearance of belief in God **53**

Chapter 8: A response to Sam Harris's *Letter to a Christian Nation* **59**

Conclusion **71**

References **73**

I

The nature of the debate

In these modern times atheism has become more and more widespread. Ever since Darwin's evolutionary theory it has become intellectually acceptable to deny the existence of God. Skepticism has become a fad in the past century and a half. About one-third of all young people between the ages of 19 and 29 are now nonbelievers. According to a nineteenth-century thinker evolution has opened wide the floodgates to perdition. Along with atheism and the rejection of God we have witnessed never before seen levels of immorality and violence in our culture. Furthermore, atheist writers have written scores of books through which they attempt to imbue in others their atheistic worldview. The public schools in America have been completely secularized, and collective, teacher led prayer has been banned and outlawed. The military has also become heavily secularized in recent years. Let us make no mistake: If the situation continues along this trajectory at the present pace, the secular government could ultimately try to eradicate Christianity from the public sphere, as was done during the Communist era in the Soviet Union, Eastern Europe, and China.

In light of the situation, a well-formed, intellectual response to atheism is necessary, demonstrating that intelligent, thinking people can indeed believe in God. This book intends to counter atheistic arguments and to present logical and intellectual proofs for the existence of God. Let us begin by describing the nature of the theist/atheist debate.

Atheism is basically a worldview that attempts to negate the existence of God (*a-theism* equates in theory to "no God"). Atheism is partially dependent upon and defined in juxtaposition to theism, basically consisting, as it does, of nothing more than a refutation of theistic arguments. This is rather obvious in the fact that many atheists spend their time mocking God, especially the triune God of the Bible (nobody ever resorts to exclamations like "Oh my Allah!" although atheists could just as well start this fad to thwart Christians). In this sense atheism is a rather empty worldview, antithetical to Christianity but offering little in place of the theistic worldview.

Let us begin by defining terms and setting goals. I would define God as the supernatural, all-knowing, all-powerful Being Who is completely apart from nature, hence "super" natural. In this debate I will seek to provide proof for the existence of such a being. While the burden of proof for the existence of God lies with the theist, it is important to note that the default setting that there is no God is unproven, begging the question underlying this dogmatic thesis. On the other hand, the onus is on the atheists to prove that nature constitutes *everything* that ever was, is, or will be, starting from the Big Bang and stretching out to the heat death of the universe.

I liken the debate to finding a white raven. Nobody has ever observed a raven of this color, since ravens are presumed, based on our experience of them, to be universally black in color. Yet no one can categorically state that white ravens do not exist; one has to but point to a single white raven and its existence will have been irrevocably established. It is at least theoretically possible that someday an explorer will emerge from the depths of some jungle, triumphantly carrying a white raven for the whole world to see. Similarly, with the existence of God, it would be sufficient for someone to bring one airtight proof for His existence and the theist-atheist debate would be over.

This debate is also like a soccer match, with theists on one team and atheists on the other. The nature of the game is that even if the atheists are ahead 79–0, a single goal for the theists would mean that they would win. And the game goes on forever, meaning that the theists can score that goal at any time. Even if the game had already come to an end and the theists still hadn't scored a single point, it still doesn't mean that they had lost.

A third way to think about the debate is by likening it to the logarithmic distribution. Consider a frog trying to cross a highway with an infinite number of lanes. With luck it just might be able to evade being hit in one, two, three, four, or even five or more lanes, but the probability steadily increases with ensuing lanes that the poor frog will be hit. If we imagine that the skeptics are particularly good at explaining away the existence of God by accounting for all observable phenomena in a natural way, the chance that they can keep on explaining away God in this way *ad infinitum* becomes less and less likely. If we imagine a conveyor belt of steadily originating theistic arguments, it is at least theoretically possible that one might eventually come that would irrefutably verify the existence of God, establishing it as reality.

It follows logically that atheists cannot legitimately be atheists but only agnostics. By the very nature of the debate itself, atheists can never conceivably win.

My intention in this book, is indeed to prove the existence of God. God (whose actuality I will assume throughout) is nonmaterial. For most atheists it is a big step to accept that anything exists in fact beyond the natural world. If we accept as intrinsic to the definition of God, as I do, that He is not only nonmaterial but also almighty, it follows that only one God can exist; we must therefore exclude polytheism (the belief in many gods) from the roster of theistic religions. If there were indeed multiple gods, one of them would have to be the principal god—the first cause, as it were.

Imagine that among multiple mathematical entities there is only one entity X, compared to which all other entities, denoted Y_i, are assumed to be smaller ($Y_i < X$). If perchance one of those other entities is in fact discovered to be larger than X, this would mean that $Y_i = X$. Therefore, polytheistic religions such as Hinduism are excluded from consideration.

It is interesting to note that even in the case of polytheistic religions there exists a main god who is often considered to be the creator of the world or the universe, such as Brahma in the Hindu religion, Zeus in Greek mythology, or Odin in Norse mythology. Still, for example in Hinduism, the 33 billion gods are all considered to be part of the natural world. The monotheistic religions such as Christianity, Judaism, and Islam all consider God to be apart from His creation.

It is vital at this juncture to define religion. A popular misconception is that religion is exclusively theistic and that atheism represents an objective worldview apart from all subjective beliefs. According to the laws of logic the negation of a statement A is itself a statement ($B = \neg A$). If we define a religious worldview as a collection of statements, then, the denial of that particular religion must also constitute a religion.

Several dictionary definitions of religion delineate the term apart from any theistic beliefs. In general, religion can be defined as a set of nonreducible axioms that cannot be proven in and of themselves but have to be assumed by faith. On this premise atheism must also count as a religion—a worldview positing the nonexistence of God. Therefore, every single human being on this planet is religious. It would be interesting, were we to press this issue, to force atheist organizations such as the Freedom From Religion Foundation (FFRF) to try to make a world without people in it.

Based upon the definition of atheism put forth by Jean-Jacque Rousseau, nature constitutes everything that ever was, is, and will be. Atheism cannot see beyond nature; by its very definition it excludes anything and everything supernatural. Many atheists believe that just because nature is all they can observe, nature accounts for all that exists; this indeed is a pivotal presupposition the proponents of atheism must be obligated to prove.

It is precisely herein that the subjective nature of atheism lies. As finite human beings we all rely upon a nonreducible set of axioms upon which we build our worldview. Contrary to the chiding of atheists against theistic reliance upon the "crutches" of religion, we simply have to make do with these crutches since we do not have all the facts (in truth, the more skeptical one is, the fewer things they can claim to "know" for sure, as we shall see later on in this book). It would be supremely arrogant to purport to know anything not based on some underlying belief or set of beliefs.

A college atheist friend of mine countered this logic by stating his belief that the structure of the universe is such that it consists of layers and layers, all of which can be known by scientific inquiry. I countered that with this very statement he was revealing his own faith premise—that everything in nature is knowable by the human mind.

The indisputable truth is that we know at best but an infinitesimally small fragment of the natural world—the minutest speck of what some might claim, humanly speaking, to be knowable. It goes without saying that no human being has ever been present throughout all time, in every corner of the galaxy, and is thereby equipped to understand everything there is to know about the natural world. My friend was dogmatic about the nature of the universe. It was his belief that we don't need belief.

Taking this to its logical conclusion, in order to make such a statement one would have to be cognizant of all there is to know in the universe—able not only to calculate in the present the precise location of every subatomic particle in the universe but to do so also with respect to both the past and the future. Such a person would be able to predict everything that would happen in the future.

The three-body problem is well known in physics. In an

extremely simplified system the behavior of two bodies (let's say two planets) can be predicted and calculated beforehand with respect to any given point in time. Interestingly, however, when a third physical body is introduced into the system the behavior of the three bodies becomes exponentially complex—so much so as to become unpredictable.

It has been estimated that there are 1088 atoms in the known universe (although it may be argued that this estimate itself relies on a number of assumptions). If some individual were able to predict the exact location of every single atom, we would have to posit that this scientist, far beyond being worthy of a Nobel prize, could only be God Himself!

Furthermore, if we take Heisenberg's uncertainty principle into account, we can never actually know the position of any particle in space. According to this principle, $\frac{h}{4}\pi \leq x \cdot m$, where x is the position of the particle, m is the momentum, h is Planck's constant $(6.63 \times 10^{-34} m2 \ kg/s)$, and $\pi \approx 3.14159$. I would challenge every atheist, here and now, to devise a program that can calculate the exact position of every particle in the universe at any given point in time. This should logically be impossible: since a computer is made up of fewer components than all of the atoms in the universe it is trying to model, it wouldn't be able to store information on each and every particle.

My college friend did in fact have extreme faith; either you exercise belief in someone who knows everything, and He is God, or you are left with unproven subjective assumptions. Atheists cannot arrive at ultimate truth, since their epistemology, which stems from their worldview, doesn't allow for it.

My primary conclusions in this chapter are not only that atheism can never win the debate but that a single proof for God would irrefutably establish His existence. Atheism, like theism, is a religion, a belief system that cannot ultimately be proven.

2

Science, knowledge, and skepticism

"Cogito ergo sum" ("I think, therefore I am"), asserted the famous French philosopher René Descartes in the seventeenth century. This single statement epitomized the nature of skepticism, carried out to its extreme form. Descartes was the ultimate skeptic in that he doubted practically everything.

A healthy dose of skepticism is actually positive. The Bible enjoins us to "prove all things; hold fast that which is good" (1 Thessalonians 5:21). However, since we humans don't know everything, the knowledge we do possess is relative. At any given time, what we have conceived to be proven truths may be refuted. Even though a thousand evidences may seem to confirm my theory, a single observation to the contrary can disprove it. As Karl Popper once observed, we can never prove a scientific theory; we can only trust it more and more. We can find more and more evidence that seems to verify a given theory, but we can never test the theory in all possible or imaginable test cases; this is something only God can do.

Descartes wanted to arrive at absolute certainty, at unconditional knowledge. The late skeptic Carl Sagan thought along the same lines. However, Descartes took skepticism to its ultimate logical conclusion by pointing out that if we doubt everything the only thing we can know for sure is that we exist, because we can be conscious only of our own thought processes. Hence his conclusion "*Cogito, ergo sum.*"

This saying has become famous, but it has little practical value and produces no knowledge whatsoever. If skeptics were to be consistent, they would have to admit that due to their own skepticism they know nothing. Skepticism inherently destroys and reduces knowledge; hence atheists like Richard Dawkins have no grounds for insulting Christians, for mocking them, as they do, as ignorant, stupid fools. In Jesus' words, "Whosoever shall say, Thou fool, shall be in danger of hell fire" (Matthew 5:21).

Carl Sagan may be commended for being self-consistent in that he advised his readers to be skeptical of the skeptics themselves. It would bring fresh air to the theist–atheist debate if atheists would only doubt the theory of evolution every now and then. This is one of my main reasons for writing this book.

Atheists act as though science were entirely on their side, confirming their worldview. But just because the objective of science is to study the natural world it doesn't mean that nature is all there is. Atheists are trapped in scientific naturalism on the basis that the scope of science deals only with nature, leaving the supernatural untouched. But the study of the supernatural, while excluded from this arena, is not thereby negated.

Science stems from the Latin *scientia*, meaning knowledge, and its goal is to increase knowledge in an orderly way. Scientific naturalism is in fact just one scientific epistemology among many. We have the freedom to choose our epistemologies, since one method may prove to be more effective than another for increasing our knowledge.

Interestingly, the Bible itself mandates scientific inquiry: "And God blessed them, and God said unto them, Be fruitful, and multiply, and replenish the earth, and *subdue it*: and *have dominion* over the fish of the sea, and over the fowl of the air, and over every living thing that moveth upon the earth" (Genesis 1:28, emphasis added). In order for humankind to subdue the earth and have dominion over it, we must acquire some working knowledge of the natural world. God entrusted the care of the natural world to human beings, not to exploit it but to tend and preserve it: "And the Lord God took the man, and put him into the garden of Eden to dress it and to keep it" (Genesis 2:15). Adam was the first taxonomist, the first to classify living things: "Out of the ground the Lord God formed every beast of the field, and every fowl of the air; and brought them unto Adam to see what he would call them: and whatsoever Adam called every living creature, that was the name thereof" (Genesis 2:19).

How do we know that Adam was capable of engaging in scientific inquiry? In Genesis 4:21–22 we read that Jubal handled harps and organs and that Tubalcain fashioned objects using brass and wood. Adam undoubtedly wasn't as technologically advanced as his successors, but according to Carl Sagan simple tribes in Africa who live close to nature prove themselves capable of pursuing science; tribesmen are obliged to study nature and the habits of animals whenever they go hunting.

At this juncture I must stress one more aspect of the picture: Even if we had in our midst one million super-intelligent, multi-Nobel-prize-winning atheist scientist professors, each with an IQ of 300, their combined intelligence and knowledge could never match those of God, the all-knowing. Since these atheists are by definition finite human beings, they must necessarily lean upon their worldview crutches. Atheists, like humans of any other persuasion, can have at best only subjective knowledge. As Popper points out, they can at best be only 99.99999999999999999999 999999999999999999% certain of what they "know." Only God can know everything, and because He created everything He can choose to reveal everything to us.

It is clear that theists have a distinct edge in the debate over atheists—the advantage revealed knowledge brings to the table. Taking this into account, we should consider it of little importance if we are mocked or scorned. We should likewise not be intimidated when seventy or so Nobel-prize-winning scientists sign a statement purporting to "know" that evolution has moved beyond theory to verifiable fact. Scientific theories by their very nature change all the time, while revealed knowledge remains the same, an unchanging, unassailable source of knowledge for all the ages.

In the absence of reliance upon revealed knowledge, the only thing we humans have left is relativism. Whereas every individual has the freedom to speculate and formulate their own theories, each is obliged to think in an effort to arrive at objective truth. Perhaps ironically, this principle is borrowed from the Protestant Reformation. As opposed to recognizing a single source of revealed, absolute truth, we are forced to acknowledge that relative truths are beyond number. Every individual is free to formulate their own body of relative truth, but when multiple, opposing "truths" are competing against each other we can be sure these formulations encompass at the same time a multitude of errors.

The main conclusion of this chapter is that skepticism, though intrinsically good, can be overdone. Skepticism ultimately destroys knowledge, and God's Word mandates the exercise of scientific inquiry. Theists have an edge over atheists in that it is possible for them to attain objective truth.

In the following chapters we will deal with concrete proofs for God, which fall into three categories: (1) proofs from creation, (2) hard evidences, as in theophanies (when God or some other supernatural agent is made known, either directly or indirectly), and (3) philosophical proofs.

3

Proofs for God from creation

Contrary to popular belief there is ample proof both for the existence of God and for the veracity of the biblical narrative. As we have seen previously, the Bible mandates engagement with science. Many intelligent scientists believe not only in God but also in the biblical story of creation. In fact, more than 600 scientists from around the world have signed a statement publicly expressing their skepticism about the theory of evolution.

Atheists understand well that one's beliefs must square with observable reality. The ability to substantiate one's viewpoint scientifically gives it the appearance of its being logical and credible. It is upon this premise that detractors attack the account of creation (and indeed the entire book of Genesis) so vehemently, claiming it to be myth. This is one of the keys to the rapid decline of Christianity following the publication of Darwin's *Origin of Species*. In Darwin's day the Church declined to engage his theory, leaving that theory to erode belief in biblical authority. A century and a half later we have seen the devastating effects of Darwinism on humankind in the forms of racism, Nazism, and Communism.

We as Christians owe it to our Creator to counterattack this atheistic undermining of the Church. Christians must use science not only to disprove evolutionary theory but also to bolster the scientific case for creation. In this way we can unravel atheism and reclaim the culture for the Bible.

History of the evolution/creation debate

It goes without saying that *scientific inquiry did not originate with Darwin*; many renowned scientists, such as the paleontologist John Owen and the biologist/geologist Louis Agassiz, predated Darwin. Darwin was unaware of the science of genetics, which was initiated by the Augustinian monk Gregor Mendel in the middle of the nineteenth century but was only met with wide acceptance by the year 1900. Prior to Darwin biologists pursued the science of natural theology, which involved distributing species into different groups that were continuous within themselves but discontinuous from each other. There were lumpers and splitters, whose task it was to draw taxonomical lines differently, depending upon how broadly or narrowly they defined a given taxonomical group. Let us not forget that the first taxonomist was Adam himself in the garden of Eden. None other than the great Swedish scholar Carolus Linnaeus, who is regarded as the father of biological taxonomy and who held the Scriptures in high regard, classified organisms into different kinds, as proposed by the book of Genesis.

Darwinian theory is portrayed by secularists as easily crushing the established theory of creation, yet this claim is simply false. The well-publicized debate between Samuel Wilberforce and Thomas Henry Huxley is portrayed as evolutionism's ultimate, crushing victory over creationism, with Wilberforce being portrayed as a simpleton churchman. In reality, numerous onlookers observed that the debate ended very nearly in a draw. No man of mean intellect, Wilberforce, the dean of Westminster, was an outstanding mathematician.

And let us not forget an earlier debate in the eighteenth century between the anatomists George Cuvier and Étienne Geoffroy

Saint-Hilaire in which Cuvier, marshaling his detailed knowledge of anatomy, refuted Saint-Hilaire's pre-evolutionary theory. The details of this earlier debate, pertinent though they were, fail to figure in to the history of the creation-evolution debate.

Creation Science

Contrary to atheist belief, creationism is indeed science. As we have seen, long before Darwin scientists investigated nature from a creationist, if not from a biblical, viewpoint. Scientific naturalism is just as subjective a viewpoint as creationism. This view, as we have seen, posits that nature constitutes everything that ever was, is, and will be; it takes the further irrational and completely unwarranted step of claiming that since science studies nature only, God cannot exist.

Although science deals with nature only, meaning that the supernatural realm and that of science do not intersect, this distinction cannot logically be taken to preclude the existence of the supernatural. According to a famous parallel, a drunken person who may have lost his keys in the dark may try to locate them under a lamp, assuming he can find them only if he sees them.

Scientific naturalism makes the further unsubstantiated claim that nature has always remained the same, without any change, implying that natural laws were identical millions of years ago to what they are now. No one can legitimately make this claim unless they indeed have existed since the beginning of time—making them, by definition, God. In contrast, according to the creation worldview, during a short period of time during creation week, not only was nature formed by God Himself through His supernatural powers, but also the laws of nature themselves.

Atheists admit the impossibility of answering the ultimate metaphysical question of why the universe came into existence, whether by random chance or as a supernatural act of God. They are left to relegate the beginning of the universe back to the realm of the unobservable—the Christian would argue that only God would have been able to observe the beginning of the universe, since He created it and was the only One present at its inception. Since a supernatural explanation for the universe is just as viable an option as a naturalistic one, why is one precluded from pursuing the science of origins in a world that, at least conceivably, has been supernaturally created? The atheists themselves are seeking to prevent a version of scientific study by claiming that creationism is unscientific.

But neither can an evolutionary theory of origins be substantiated in the same verifiable way as gravity or the laws of thermodynamics. The law of gravity can be tested over and over again—with an identical, predictable result. But phylogeny, the theory of a macroevolutionary development of species from the first primordial cell all the way to the human being, cannot be observed, let alone tested even once. Evolution, unlike gravity, is rightfully defined as a theory. Evolutionists can only work with models, a process that involves speculating with dozens or hundreds, if not thousands, of different parameters. Models do not become reality just because conclusions based on their behavior may sound convincing and neat. Evolutionary models, while describing *how* species *could have* evolved over millions of years, do not prove *that* they have actually done so. Herein lies the key distinction between scientific fact and speculation.

Evolutionary theory is subjective and non-scientific in that it depends absolutely upon the assumptions of lengthy ages and gradual and nonmaterial processes. Furthermore, it has never been, and indeed cannot be, observed.

According to the creation worldview there is an inherent order in creation. This is because God as a super intelligent, supernatural Being would have it so. Scientific inquiry is all about discovering order in nature as a vital step toward establishing natural laws.

Since God is the Creator, the believer would argue, He is also the Intelligent Designer of the universe. Atheists may rail against the assertion of Intelligent Design, yet it too has a scientific basis. Archeology is the study of ancient cultures, including Egyptology, which deciphers hieroglyphs and ancient writings. Thus mathematics, logic, and linguistics are all involved in deciphering ancient writings and uncovering their meaning. These endeavors are fully as scientific as physics, biology, or geology. Archeology operates from the presupposition that ancient hieroglyphs were created by human intelligence—without positing anything about the nature of the intelligence behind the hieroglyphs. By the same principle, it is also legitimate to say that by studying nature, such as DNA, for example, we can see the handiwork of God.

Scientists have spent decades of intense research trying to determine the meaning of genes and non-coding DNA. Decades ago, according to evolutionary theory, the larger part of the genome was designated as functionless, "junk" DNA; the functioning part of the genome was seen to reside in the genes that code for enzymes, channels, or regulatory proteins. "The one gene, one function" thesis predominated at that time. However, with scientific progress many new functions have been found in the non-coding part of the DNA, formerly designated as evolutionary junk. The mere existence of junk DNA is implausible, since the organism, according to evolutionary theory, would streamline its own genome (imagine making a copy of a book that is mostly junk; you would waste a lot of paper and ink in the process).

Thermodynamics and the Big Bang

According to materialistic theories, the universe expanded from a very small, dense particle. The question is, naturally, how long that particle existed before exploding in the Big Bang to bring the universe into existence. Assuming that this Big Bang particle had existed forever, stretching back infinitely into the past, would be meaningless. Yet this is precisely the claim of atheists like Carl Sagan, some of whom talk about an oscillating universe that continuously expands and then collapses, like a perpetuum mobile, forever. This is impossible, because an eternity of time would have to come to pass before the present moment. Furthermore, such perpetuum mobile constructs do not in fact exist because they would be slowed down by friction. This also means that an eternally expanding and contracting universe would eventually come to a grinding halt.

Big Bang theories contradict the well-grounded laws of thermodynamics, which state that order continuously decreases as entropy, or dis-order, continuously increases. Order, we know, does not arise from disorder. According to some materialistic cosmologies the universe will someday die a heat death because it will no longer have free energy to sustain any processes. Thus cosmological evolution takes us from an initial state of less order to a state of progressively higher order, ultimately ending up once again in a state of less order, which is highly contradictory. Thermodynamics is an obstacle for evolutionary theory, and some evolutionists have attempted to discredit it, despite its being a fundamental law of physics.

The first cell

An interesting aspect of cell biology is identification of the minimal organism—an organism that has the smallest possible number of genes to remain viable and capable of independent existence, meaning that it is able to produce its own nutrients to maintain its own system. It is important that this first, primordial cell be capable of independent existence; if it were a parasite it would necessarily need another, more developed organism off which to live.

A multitude of organisms have been listed as candidates for the position of minimal organism. Many of these have very small genomes; some are less than 1 Mbp in size and have only several hundred genes. Yet many of these are in fact parasites; an example is the bacterium *Mycoplasma genitalium*, which has a genome of 540 genes and about 500 Kbp (kilo base pairs).

It is ultimately impossible to determine which species might count as the minimal organism, since life supposedly evolved more than a billion years ago. Yet this does not deter evolutionists from speculation. According to some models the minimal organism contained around 1,340 genes. If an average protein contains 100 amino acids, and there are 50,000 possible protein families, the probability of a single protein being viable is $5\times10^4/20^{100} \approx 3.9\times10^{-126}$. Thus the probability that all of the proteins were viable at once in the first cell is $(3.9\times10^{-126})^{1340} \approx 10^{-167,500}$. This probability is beyond imagination, an obstacle impossible for the theory of evolution to surmount.

Some evolutionists claim that the tree of life is more like a bush at its base. This is because life could conceivably have arisen at multiple times and in multiple locations all across the globe. Genes could have been interchanged among these early cellular life forms, greatly accelerating the rate of evolution. This seems plausible at first, but the theory suffers from an insurmountable problem, that of homochirality. Homochirality means that the amino acids that make up the proteins within cells are all of one type, either left- or right-handed.

An amino acid is left- or right-handed according to how the hydrogen and the side chain are oriented on the alpha carbon in the amino acid. An amino acid can be depicted with the formula $C-(H)C_{alpha}(R)-N$ if it is left-handed, or $C-(R)C_{alpha}(H)-N$ if it is right-handed (see Figure 1), where R is the side chain of the amino acid. It is interesting that every amino acid of every single living being has the same handedness; hence, homochirality. The probability that every single primordial cell would have manifested the same handedness is so infinitely small that it is practically zero. Evolutionary theory doesn't stand a chance in this argument.

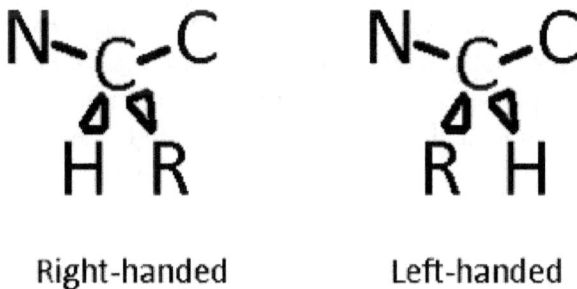

Right-handed   Left-handed

Figure 1 - Chirality

On mutations

Mutations are the driving force behind evolution. The basic steps presumed to be taken during natural selection are the following: first, a mutation happens within the genome—all of the DNA of a given species, meaning all bases in all of its chromosome(s). By mutation we generally mean any kind of change, great or small, that occurs within the genome. A mutation can either be silent, or synonymous, if no phenotypic change occurs (an organism's phenotype entails all inward and outward physical characteristics), or non-synonymous if it changes the protein that the gene encodes. Different classes of mutations include base pair substitutions, insertions, deletions, chromosomal rearrangements, and duplications.

Simple base pair mutations affect only one base pair and generally don't have much of an effect. A substitution, for example, happens when cytosine becomes an adenine $(C \rightarrow A)$. A base pair substitution can change an amino acid if the new codon (base triplet) codes for a different amino acid. If an amino acid changes it can potentially destroy the protein structure. This can happen if one of the amino acids in the enzyme's active center (the part of the enzyme responsible for catalyzing a reaction) is replaced. This is due to the specialized side chains hanging out from the protein's backbone. In sickle-cell anemia, for example, the protein hemoglobin is structurally rearranged in such a way that the red blood cell is deformed and incapable of carrying oxygen to the tissues.

Frameshift mutations are even more destructive. As mentioned earlier, a base triplet codes for a single amino acid. However, if a single base pair is either removed from or inserted into the gene, all of the amino acids after the mutation will be changed—shifted either up or down by one base pair, causing the protein to be truncated.

Insertional mutations occur when foreign genetic elements are inserted into an existing gene. For example, transposons or mobile genetic elements may land smack-dab into the middle of a gene, thereby destroying the sequence (the same thing that happens in a frameshift mutation). A deletion has the same effect, except that here DNA is deleted. Different size insertions and/or deletions may occur, ranging from just a few base pairs to thousands.

Chromosomal rearrangements occur when larger sections of chromosomes are translocated from one place to another. These mutations may seem to be neutral, since there is no net loss or gain of genetic material. However, the translocation break may occur in the middle of a gene. Furthermore, genes on different chromosomes may take part in the same process and thus might be induced at the same time. Sometimes parts of different chromosomes may come physically closer to each other in order to undergo simultaneous genetic regulation (such genetic elements are called distal enhancers). Naturally, if part of a chromosome has been translocated, this regulation is therefore disrupted.

Finally, there are genetic duplications. Evolutionists bank heavily upon this process as an explanation for the genesis of new genes from raw sequences. The theory goes that if a chromosome segment is duplicated, the gene exists in two separate copies. One is retained, while the other is free to mutate into another gene. However, this model has inherent problems.

For example, 75% of all such duplications are subsequently lost. Also, it isn't always good for the organism for an enzyme to suddenly be present in a doubled amount. Several cellular processes involve steps that are catalyzed by enzymes that need to be present in exactly the amounts needed. If the quantity changes, the catalytic process suffers imbalance. This is why chromosomal duplications have such a deleterious effect in Down syndrome.

Plant scientists also point out that polyploid plants (plants with multiplied whole genomes) are rarely viable and constitute evolutionary dead-ends. Even if individual genes can duplicate, the chance that a random stretch of DNA can mutate by chance into a meaningful new gene is extremely low. All of the base pairs in the new gene would have to mutate in the right direction simultaneously.

For the most part mutations either do not bring about new

characteristics or cause the loss of genetic material. In some cases the loss of genetic material can cause new characteristics to emerge. These include the loss of inhibition factors. This produces, in effect, a double negative: If the inhibition of a given gene itself is inhibited, this causes a certain characteristic to be expressed. The gene coding for the seemingly new characteristic had always been in the genome but had previously been stifled by an inhibitory regulator protein. If the gene for this inhibitory protein is deleted from the genome, the first gene is free to be expressed.

Gradualism, "punk-eek," and creationism compared

According to the theory of evolution all species are interconnected in the evolutionary tree. This means that all of life, all species, and even all organisms are interrelated, since all life is posited to have come from a single cell or set of cells (which, as we have seen in the previous subchapter, is virtually impossible). The idea that all species have derived from a single proto-organism is a massive problem for evolutionary theory, unless evolutionists are willing to concede that all humans evolved from a single pair of parents (Adam and Eve), as creation theory holds. If humans are not assumed to have evolved from a single pair of parents, it is much more difficult to explain how all of life could have derived from a single cell.

But this is exactly what evolutionary theory purports. There are two primary approaches to how species evolve over time. Gradual evolution, as espoused by Dawkins, posits that species accrue infinitesimally small mutations over time, with each newly evolved species differing ever so slightly from its parent species. Gradualism fits well with observations from genetics, in that mutations mainly cause only the slightest modifications in the offspring. However, the theory does not fit well with the evidence from paleontology, which shows that there are many large gaps in the fossil record. In general, paleontologists find that each new fossil can either be classified as an existing kind of organism or must be assigned its own group if it doesn't resemble any known species.

Punctuated equilibrium, or the "punk-eek" theory, as espoused by the late Marxist Stephen J. Gould, along with Niles Eldridge, states that under certain circumstances species undergo rapid evolution, thus leaving very few intermediate forms. In other words, species remain for a time in stasis or equilibrium, punctuated by rapid species change. The punk-eek theory fits well with the gaps in the fossil evidence (that is why it was formulated), although we must add that negative evidence (missing fossils) carries much less weight than positive evidence, not to mention that the theory only poorly explains the genetics data. Some genetics theories that are floating around attempt to explain how certain genetic elements or structures undergo rapid mutations, but these hypotheses can hardly be supported by the evidence.

In sum, the theory of gradualism fares well in genetics but fits only poorly with evidence from the fossil record. Punk-eek, on the other hand, explains the fossil evidence but fits poorly with genetics. However, we can turn to a third theory, which explains both genetics and the fossil record quite satisfactorily. According to creation species theory, God created organisms as members of different "kinds": "And God said, Let the earth bring forth the living creature after his kind, cattle, and creeping thing, and beast of the earth after his kind: and it was so" (Genesis 1:24) This suggests that there are gaps between distinct kinds.

While there is genetic continuity among members of a kind, there is discontinuity among kinds. Organisms representing two different kinds are wholly unrelated to one another. Examples of kinds are cats, dogs, horses, pigeons, and humankind. Cats will always remain cats; they will never transform into dogs. This theory is called baraminology, deriving from the combining of a Hebrew with a Greek word: אָרָב (barah) means to create, while λογος (logos) signifies knowledge. Creation theory, then, far from denying speciation (the creation of new species), accommodates it. The different created kinds form an orchard of interrelated species (see Figure 2).

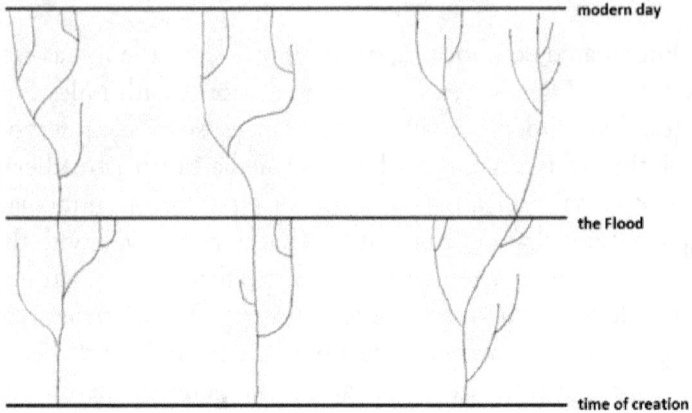

modern day

the Flood

time of creation

Figure 2 – The creation species concept

This has interesting, though difficult, ramifications for evolutionary theory, which was obviously formulated without having observed macroevolution all the way from the earliest cells to modern humans. Darwin inferred the total inter-relatedness of all species from observing modern species. He simply assumed that the fossil record would bear out his theory of gradual, intermediary evolutionary steps. As we have seen, it did not; hence the introduction of punk-eek theory. There are several wide transitions or leaps in biological evolution that have given evolutionists headaches in trying to explain. These troublesome areas include life from nonlife, DNA-based life from RNA-based life, eukaryotes from prokaryotes, multicellular organisms from single-cell organisms, triploblasty, vertebrates from non-vertebrates, amphibians from fish, humans from nonhumans, and solitary individuals to colonies. These transitions necessarily involve mutations in dozens, if not hundreds, of genes. The transition, for example, from invertebrates to vertebrates would have had to involve the inversion of the organism's entire body plan.

If Christians engaged in the sciences could convincingly prove that at least one such transition did not occur (this could be any transition from one species to another, not just major steps), the entire theory of evolution would be disproven. If we look at

Figure 3, the implication is that if one sub-tree is cut off from the main tree (represented by an X), the sub-tree could only have come about by non-evolutionary means. For example, if the cut were between birds and reptiles, the assumption would have to be made that birds emerged in a void, which is completely ludicrous; there could be no natural explanation for that—*only a supernatural one*. On this basis we would be obliged to assert that God exists.

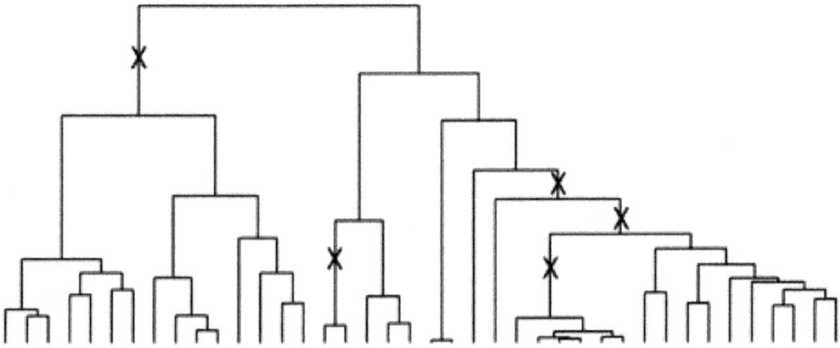

Figure 3 - Proving all links in the evolutionary tree

If we count the first single cell as the root of the evolutionary tree, branching off into two daughter species, the result will be a binary tree with $2^{k+1}-1$ transitions, if k represents the number of evolutionary steps leading from the first cell to any of today's modern species (the trees on the evolutionary tree). Each of these transitions needs to be explained satisfactorily by evolutionary theory.

If there are 1000 genes in the first living organism and 31,000 genes in *Daphnia pulex*, the species with the largest number of genes, we are left with a difference of 30,000 genes. This means that 30,000 steps separate this modern species from that first cell. Thus there are $2^{30,000}-1 \approx 10^{9,000}$ branches in the evolutionary tree. Even if evolutionists could satisfactorily explain, with 99.9% accuracy, the transition across all branches in this tree, the probability that all transitions can be accounted for is $0.999^{10^{1000000}}$ something even scientific calculators cannot calculate. When asked to provide but a single observed example of evolution happening between different kinds of organisms, evolutionists are generally stumped.

Evolutionary conservation and genome decay

The field of genomics provides outstanding support for creation theory. If the theory of evolution is true, it is required that massive amounts of genetic material be added to the genome. Further, we humans would have to have gotten our lowly start from the first independent living cell (a premise for which we have seen that the probability is extremely low, around $10^{-167,500}$), which would have had about 1000 genes in a genome of around 1 Mbp, and purely through different classes of mutations have arrived at the human genome, which is 3 Gbp and has around 20,000 genes, all within the timespan of around one billion years. In other words, purely by rewriting, shifting, deleting, and adding the letters A, C, G, and T, we should be able to transform the genome of the first cell into the human genome. Imagine for a moment a naked genome, passing its way through millions of intermediary species between the first cell and the human species. The reason we are able to view the genome in this way is that the genotype (defined as all the genes in the genome) determines the phenotype. Without the genotype the phenotype is meaningless. This hypothetical process is illustrated in Figure 4.

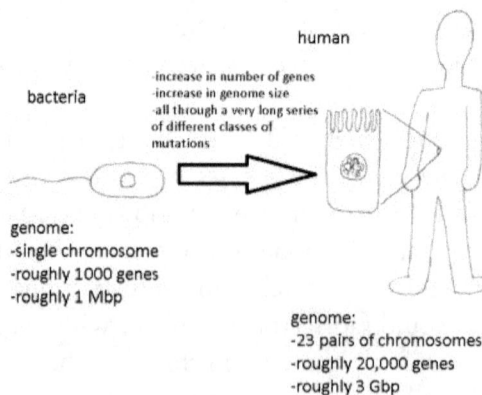

human

bacteria

·increase in number of genes
·increase in genome size
·all through a very long series
 of different classes of
 mutations

genome:
-single chromosome
-roughly 1000 genes
-roughly 1 Mbp

genome:
-23 pairs of chromosomes
-roughly 20,000 genes
-roughly 3 Gbp

Figure 4 – Evolutionary demands on increase in amount of genetic material from early cell to human being

Furthermore, it would make logical sense that as we progress through evolution, older genes would be lost from the genome as newer genes are acquired—formed from random genetic sequences. This is similar to species arising during evolution and then at some later point going extinct. In other words, both species and genes should have an evolutionary lifespan.

As we have seen in a previous subchapter, evolution via different classes of mutation is incapable of producing new genetic material—new genes. Horizontal gene transfer may be capable of bringing in new genes between different species, but this possibility decreases as an organism becomes more complex. This does in fact happen frequently in bacteria, which do not even have a nuclear membrane, whereas eukaryotes do have a nuclear membrane, as well as cellular wall structures.

Interestingly, there are two widespread phenomena within living organisms that completely contradict genomic evolution. The first is evolutionary conservation. Pause for a moment to consider the two words that make up this compound term. Evolution denotes change, development, or mutation from one state to another, while conservation implies the exact opposite, suggesting that a genomic structure freezes up and remains unchanged over time. The term "evolutionary conservation," is, then, an oxymoron, a paradox. It describes well how existing genetic structures retain their function and also explains these structures' resistance to change. This is because the nature of mutations is to destabilize or destroy an existing genetic structure. It is also remarkable that genes' lifespans are different from those of species during evolution. In other words, besides evolutionary conservation there is early complexity.

For example, the genome of an amoeba species, *Amoeba dubia*, has a size of 670 Gbp, more than 223 times larger than the human genome. If we look at cnidarians (a phylum which is made up of species of jellyfish and anemones), which is close to the evolutionary tree of animals, just after protists, placozoans, and sponges, we see that they have genes responsible for neuronal development that are conserved in animals all the way up to humans. Cnidarians also exhibit courting and predatory behavior; have a sense of balance; and, in some species, such as *Tripedalia*, have double eyes with retinas, lenses, and mobile irises. Even single-celled protists have a camera-type eye structure, together with a retina-like structure and a lens, such as is seen in the family *Warnowiaceae*. Cnidarians also are triploblastic, meaning that they have three basic germ cell lines: ectoderm for an outer body covering; endoderm for the lining of the intestine; and mesoderm, which is responsible for the production of muscles and internal organs.

Not only are genomic structures conserved, but they also undergo size reduction. Some evolutionary theories state that mammalian genomes came about from reptile genomes via reduction. I would speculate that it is the inherent nature of the material universe to devolve, as opposed to evolving, as is purported in evolutionary theory. Not only does entropy increase due to thermodynamics, but genomes tend to decrease in size and lose genes through pseudogenization (a process during which certain genes lose their function). As an interesting sidenote, languages too tend to simplify over time, become generalized, and lose grammatical constructs; this can be seen in the German→Dutch→Afrikaans trajectory.

Such a process is widespread within different genera of bacterial species, such as those of *Bordetella*, *Mycobacterium*, and *Yersinia*. Typical of this phenomenon is that the initial species in the wild have genomes that are larger in size and have more genes than subsequent species. In subsequent species pseudogenes accrue, insertions and deletions occur, and the genome gets scrambled up, with bits and pieces falling out here and there. Genome size also shrinks. Eventually, certain species within the genus may colonize a host organism, such as aphids or other insects. Since they are at that point inside a host organism, which supplies them with ready nutrients, there is less pressure for these parasitic bacteria to retain those genes within their genome that help produce that specific nutrient. Instead they become dependent upon the host. Furthermore, bacteria may lose genes responsible for certain surface proteins that help evade the immune system. Bacterial genomes may become so reduced that they become endosymbionts that are tightly attached to their host organisms. Endosymbionts are different from cell organelles in that bacteria have a positive gene to genome size correlation; for organelles this correlation is negative.

All in all, genome reduction is a phenomenon consistent with creation theory—devolution from a common monophyletic ancestor species—as opposed to evolution. Whereas genome reduction may fit evolutionary theory, it ultimately doesn't prove it, but is actually opposite of genome inflation, which is needed to explain evolution.

Living fossils

Living fossils are species that are alive today despite being thought to have gone extinct long ago. Such species have remained virtually unchanged for long periods of evolutionary time, as long as millions of years. Their environment has somehow remained unchanged during all this time, allowing for them to remain unchanged as well.

Although such species may be expected to be rare, they are surprisingly common. Hundreds and even thousands have been discovered across all taxonomic groups.

The best-known living fossil is the *Coelecanth*, which was believed to have lived 400 million years ago but was discovered in 1938 in the Indian Ocean. Contrary to evolutionary expectations, it had no primitive lungs but only fatty tissue. The platypus, another living fossil, was believed to have gone extinct 166 million years ago, and trilobites have supposedly inhabited this earth for 445 million years. The *Nautilus*, a common index fossil, has supposedly existed for 500 million years, while the snapping turtle, *Chelydra serpentina*, a reptile, has purportedly existed for 215 million years. Alligators and crocodiles are believed to have existed for 60 million years; the goblin shark, *Mitsukurina owstoni*, for 120 million years;

and the mouse deer, *Tragulus nepu*, for 35 million years.

A more likely explanation is that these living fossils didn't continuously exist for millions of years. The world's environments change regularly, forcing species to adapt at an accelerated rate. Since some of these species are ubiquitous (such as the Nautilus and Trilobites, which have remained unchanged throughout much of the Earth's existence), it is much more likely that they are not millions of years old but relatively young, conforming to a young age of the Earth, as predicated by the Bible.

Summary

My main conclusion of this chapter is that mutations do occur in nature and that news species do come about, but only within limitations. Genes and species are constant throughout time. Creation is the most plausible theory by which to explain speciation. The evolution of the first cell is practically zero. Increase in evolutionary complexity is impossible, as devolution, not evolution, is the predominant trend in nature. Devolution can also be observed in physics. Even supposedly simple organisms have complex organs, which early evolutionary theory did not assume to have existed.

4

Theophanies and spiritual manifestations

Many an atheist has exclaimed that if God does indeed exist, it would only make sense for Him to show Himself to us—a physical manifestation of God in the natural world would be sufficient proof of His presence. I have lived in both America and Europe and have had the opportunity to speak with many different people representing numerous languages and diverse worldviews. The reality is that such theophanies or spiritual manifestations have indeed occurred. I hasten to caution the reader, however, that we are not encouraged to seek for a physical sign of God but rather to study the Word, the sole authority in defining truth.

I define theophany or spiritual manifestation as an event during which a supernatural being outside of nature comes into contact with or influences processes within the natural world, either directly or indirectly. There are several different kinds of theophanies or spiritual manifestations. Many such stories have been told within the Church; they can be heard from time to time, both from missionaries and from laypersons. Skeptics will naturally be cynical about such miraculous events; this attitude stems from their subjective worldview. However, whereas we infer the existence of God from creation, spiritual manifestations or thophanies are direct proofs of God's existance, which directly contradict the legitimacy of their perspective.

While it cannot be denied that some of these reports are falsifiable or outright deceptions, some phenomena have been misunderstood, and some people may have been in the throes of psychological trauma, other accounts are so plain as to be undeniable. Further, even if we can offer a natural explanation for most of these events, it would be sheer prejudice to state patently that everybody who claims a supernatural encounter or experience is insane, deceptive, or stupid.

Some atheists claim that it is much more likely that someone who reports having seen a miracle is a liar than for the purported miracle to actually have happened. This reasoning is nonsensical; it is impossible to calculate the probability of a miracle happening because probability is a discipline of mathematics, a tool of the natural sciences. Such logic would be like comparing apples to oranges. Probability works by calculating the ratio of desirable outcomes against all possible outcomes. These results have to be observable and repeatable—subject, that is, to the laws of nature and the tools of science.

Atheists themselves confirm that natural science does not consider the supernatural; therefore one cannot use probability as a tool to describe it. Furthermore, if atheists reject miracles out of hand (based on their worldview bias), the probability of any miracle having happened, according to them, is zero. If they presuppose that miracles cannot and do not happen, this is precisely the point to which their conclusions will lead them. They cannot have it both ways. Still, I would contest that the statement that miracles are highly unlikely leaves them with a non-zero probability. On the other hand, according to evolutionary rhetoric, if we wait long enough to hear a substantially large number of reports about miracles, purely by the law of large numbers we are forced to accept that at least some miracles have likely occurred.

In the following section I have compiled a record of some of the supernatural events and manifestations about which I have heard during my life as a Christian.

Charismatic phenomena

I will first examine the charismatic churches, which claim that the Holy Spirit moves directly upon people. There can be no doubt that some of these claims are bogus. For example, I tried my best to explain to a charismatic girl whom I met on Facebook that Jesus' face wasn't literally visible on a sheet of snow covering her car's windshield. She had taken a photo, and we'd had a lengthy discussion about whether or not it was or really Jesus' physiognomy etched there in the snow. I referred to verses from the Bible that I felt contradicted the validity of this apparent phenomenon: "Thou shalt not make unto thee any graven image, or any likeness of any thing that is in heaven above, or that is in the earth beneath, or that is in the water under the earth" (Exodus 20:4). Clearly, I countered, if God directed us not to depict Him in any kind of image He would not portray Himself in any such physical way. Furthermore, my friend claimed that Jesus had long hair in the snowy image on the windshield, an apparent contradiction of 1 Corinthians 11:14: "Doth not even nature itself teach you, that, if a man have long hair, it is a shame unto him?" God does not contradict Himself in the Bible compared to what we see in reality.

In another instance Sándor Németh of the Hungarian Faith Movement (Hit Gyülekezet) directed one of the maintenance personnel at his church to turn up the fans above the congregation full blast during the following Sunday's sermon so that they could "experience the Holy Spirit among them."

Many people claim to have been healed by faith preachers who have laid hands on them. The great majority of these ostensible healings, in my considered opinion, are not real. If they were indeed real, these faith healers could go into hospital buildings and heal every sick person, virtually putting the medical profession out of business.

Finally, although it has become popular among charismatic church people, the movie "Heaven Is for Real" is in fact far from real—so much so that the main actor, a young boy, expressed grief that the movie was leading so many people astray from the truth.

Despite such travesties, however, I am convinced that something otherworldly does indeed often happen during the course of charismatic church services. Many people report having been "slain in the spirit" and lying paralyzed for hours on end, sometimes even standing frozen like a statue for several days—if they were faking it, they would surely have had to go to the bathroom. Others report having been able to see the outside world after closing their eyes and being able to walk down a church aisle without bumping into anything. Still other reports include people walking off the edge of a stage while being suspended in the middle of the air. Many of these events happen in churches with packed crowds, with an ample number of witnesses present to verify these things.

I see this last as a vivid example of suspension of the natural law of gravity. If the report is reliable, something supernatural has indeed occurred. Only something greater than a natural phenomenon could suspend natural processes; the lesser has no power over the greater, but only vice-versa.

Many, including Muslims in Middle Eastern countries where the Christian faith is suppressed, report having seen graphic visions. While some of these accounts might be valid, in my mind this a gray area. My charismatic professor colleague reported to me a vision of a gigantic menorah representing the different branches of the Church, symbolizing in his mind the importance of the various Christian denominations holding together. This was no unlearned man but a biology professor who had written 50 papers by the time he was 36 and who took part in biology conferences. A thoroughgoing skeptic beforehand, he had gone so far as to persecute the Church. This particular example would be hard for skeptics to explain away.

This professor friend of mine also reported having witnessed one of his family members drinking several gallons of water without becoming bloated. In Norse mythology something similar happened when King Útgarða-Loki informed the hero,

Þór, that his warrior giants were able to empty a drinking horn filled with liquid. The common element in these stories strikes me as rather peculiar in that it transcends not only geographic locations but also centuries.

My Hebrew teacher, who also works as a dental technician in my city of residence, recounted to me the story of his conversion to Christianity, claiming that a great wind had swept through one of the rooms in his house. The pages of his Bible were left fluttering, and he heard voices reciting Isaiah 6:3: "Holy, holy, holy, is the Lord of hosts: the whole earth is full of his glory." My Hebrew teacher is a kind and intelligent man who is certainly not insane, slow-witted, or deluded.

I hosted a girl on one occasion from an internet couch-surfing website. Charismatic by persuasion, she talked about her experiences, informing me that when she closes her eyes while enraptured in prayer she sees Jesus. I shared with her that in Hungary many gypsies are superstitious and delve into the occult. One social worker reported that a gypsy boy had complained to her that he continuously sees his dead mother when he closes his eyes. The parallel to this girl's report struck me as strange and disconcerting.

Yet another class of supernatural events is that of speaking in tongues, or *glossolalia*. I personally have heard charismatics speak in tongues multiple times. Twice I witnessed the phenomenon during two different charismatic church services in Hungary. This is the only kind of purportedly supernatural event I have experienced firsthand. In both instances more than a dozen people were present, making me doubt that every tongue speaker was demented or disingenuous. Two of my intellectual charismatic friends have also claimed to speak in tongues—one of them a professor and the other a student of mathematics while I was in college.

There are supposedly several varieties of glossolalia. One supposedly allows a speaker to speak in a foreign language without having learned it. According to other charismatics, when they speak in tongues they are speaking not in human languages but in "angelic" tongues, uninterpretable by human beings. Since 1901, when the Kansas City Prophets first started re-experiencing this biblical Pentecostal phenomenon, glossolalia has become widespread in the charsmatic churches. I personally suspect that it is for the most part a psychosomatic phenomenon. For some, speaking in tongues can seem like a special mystical experience, and by having this experience they can be part of the in-group in these churches. Therefore by speaking meaningless words rapidly they even fool themselves into believing that they also can speak in tongues.

Strangely enough, when I have asked my charsmatic friends to refrain from speaking in tongues they appeared capable of curbing these impulses. They seem to have exerted some sort of power over the Holy Spirit—if this were indeed the case, I could only determine that this glossolalia was not of God since one cannot, according to Christian theology, limit the Holy Spirit.

Despite this reservation, I must concede that some occurrences of glossolalia appear not to constitute a sham. For example, my mathematician friend also reported having experienced „fire baptism," which he describes as a warm feeling running up and down his body. Others have reported speaking in tongues in such a manner that they have lost control over their bodies, with their jaws moving up and down against their will. Unfortunately, I can't help but wonder, at least in some cases, whether this might be a manifestation of demonic possession.

Peculiar coincidences

Missionaries to African and Asian countries at times report spiritual or even demonic manifestations. One missionary to an African country was present when a witch doctor began lifting one hand into the air, followed by a leg and then the other hand. Ultimately he started dancing in the air, with none of his limbs touching the ground, evidently lifted by some unseen force. Along the same line, a friend of mine who spent some time in India witnessed a woman who was able to speak unnaturally with a deep male voice—a possible instance of demonic possession.

When I lived in Hungary we would sometimes travel from our church to neighboring Transylvania, which had belonged to Hungary before the end of World War I but is now a part of Romania. There we met a man in a village who continuously swore. This man ended up suffering a stroke and was unable from that point on to speak. Possibly divine punishment for foul language? Or what about the story our pastor told us about a man who challenged God that he would believe in Him only if he were permitted to shake hands with Him. Later on his wife gave birth to a baby who was missing both hands.

In 1 Kings 17:1–6 we read the story of Elijah, who was being chased by the wicked queen Jezabel and was hiding in the Kerith Ravine. Elijah lived during a time of frequent miraculous intervention in human affairs, and in this instance God ordered ravens to come and feed the prophet while he was hiding. Sound miraculous enough? My question at this point is whether this kind of divine mediation still happens today. It could. A Hungarian pastor was removed from his church during the dark era of Communism and forced to live near some ruins by the Black Sea. The house didn't even have a roof! Upon their arrival he and his wife had nothing to eat. Suddenly they saw an animal coming toward them from the woods—a wolf carrying a loaf of bread in its mouth.

Similarly, a pastor friend of mine told several of us during a Bible study that while he was in Ethiopia he had witnessed a truck driver being ordered to run over a Christian man who was lying on the ground. He drove the truck forward, but it was stopped as though by some invisible force. He backed up and tried again, only to be halted a second time. After experiencing this outcome yet a third time, he jumped from the truck and ran away.

The innate knowledge of God

"To h—— with their culture," blurted Richard Dawkins during an interview with Bill Maher on HBO in November 2015. He was criticizing Islam for forcing women to wear burkhas. Beyond the question of why Dawkins would presume to know what is best for others despite presumably avowing cultural relativism, this strikes me to be an example of an avowed atheist somehow possessing an innate knowledge of God. What, other than divine compulsion, might have compelled Dawkins to make a rude statement in a rash moment about sending Islamic culture to a supernatural dimension?

Counterintuitive though this may seem, research from social psychology has shown that some atheists interpret important life events as teleo-functional occurrences, allowing for the presence of some superintelligent Being behind the scenes, guiding the events. Atheists have also been known to consider prayer when confronted with an extremely difficult situation. Other instances have been reported of avowed atheists refusing to sign a contract whereby they would ostensibly sell their souls to the experimenter, even if the contract itself were entirely meaningless. A study has found that in a test group composed of a combination of theists and atheists, both groups were apt to associate supernatural beings with existential questions when forced to think deeply about their own deaths.

These remarkable results attest to the fact that all people are, at least on a subconscious level, aware of the existence of God, the truth of which is indelibly written upon their hearts and minds: "For when the Gentiles, which have not the law, do by nature the things contained in the law, these, having not the law, are a law unto themselves: Which shew the work of the law written in their hearts, their conscience also bearing witness, and their thoughts the mean while accusing or else excusing one another" (Romans 2:14–15).

Jesus Christ

I see as the most irrefutable proof for God's existence the historical record of the birth, life, death, and resurrection of Jesus Christ, the Son of God who voluntarily took upon Himself human flesh and deigned to dwell among us. In the previous chapter we have seen the manner in which creation science supports the Bible, the only reliable source of truth. Jesus performed many signs and miracles demonstarting that He was more than just a man. The Jewish historian Josephus records that many people in His time thought of Jesus as someone divine from heaven.

Summary

Many atheists in their heart of hearts long for a sign verifying the existence of God. They want to grasp Him with their minds, even though God cannot be forced under a microscope. In Matthew 16:4 Jesus Himself is recorded as saying, "A wicked and adulterous generation seeketh after a sign; and there shall no sign be given unto it, but the sign of the prophet Jonas." God wants each of us to seek a personal relationship with Himself. First and foremost, He yearns for us to seek Him in His Word in order to understand His truth. If anyone seeks God in earnest, He will reveal Himself to them.

5

Why is there suffering?

This question is absolutely relevant to the debate about the existence of God, not to mention that it affects each of us in the most poignant, personal way. Pain and suffering are ubiquitous and unavoidable in this world. Many atheists rightly surmise that if God does exist He must be as good as it would be possible to be. If God is good, they further speculate—in this case misguidedly—He would not allow anyone to suffer. Atheists who reason this way find themselves caught in a Catch 22; they conjecture, based on the reality of pain, that if God does exists He must not be good. If, on the other hand, God is good, He must not exist.

But this is human logic, which God is infinitely above. In fact, it bypasses entirely the reality and significance of God's existence. God's presence on the human scene and the reality of suffering don't follow from each other in what we would deem to be a logical manner. God's purposes for allowing human pain might, in fact, be far different from what even we as Christians might imagine.

In order for us to get a handle on the why of suffering in this world, it is necessary to understand the Christian worldview, as depicted in Figure 5. It is important here to stress that God's original creation was

The eternal state
GOOD: no sin,
pain, death
man in relationship
with God again

(lasts forever)

Jesus comes again
Final Judgement

The Millenium

Jesus on the cross

Resurrection
Ascension

Flood (First Judgement)

BAD: pain, death, suffering, sin (temporary)

Creation
Fall into Sin

GOOD: no sin,
pain, death
man in
relationship
with God

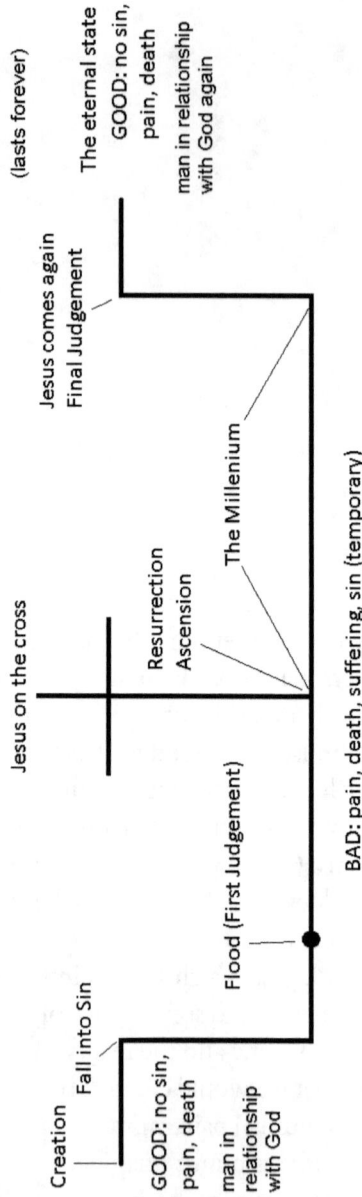

Figure 5 - The Christian worldview

good and that though suffering is bad, it is only temporary. Jesus died on the cross on behalf of sinful humanity to undo the stain of the sin that Adam and Eve had committed in the garden of Eden (Romans 5:12–20). Jesus lived a perfect and righteous life, and His sinlessness is now imputed to us, just as our sins have been transferred in God's eyes to the account of Jesus. Jesus Christ will come again at the end of time to judge the living and the dead and to put an end once and for all to suffering and death; He will also create a new heavens and a new earth, liberated at last from the effects of sin (Romans 8:21–22).

Matthew 9:1–3 illuminates this issue: "As Jesus passed by, he saw a man which was blind from his birth. And his disciples asked him, saying, Master, who did sin, this man, or his parents, that he was born blind? Jesus answered, Neither hath this man sinned, nor his parents: but that the works of God should be made manifest in him."

It is enlightening here to glimpse an aspect of the Jewish mentality. The Jews of Jesus' day viewed illness, disability, or pain as punishment from God. They were correct in attributing the origins of suffering and death to the actions of our first parents, Adam and Eve. As a direct result of the curse women of all times have borne their children in pain (Genesis 3:16). Men—and women—are obliged to work hard for their bread against natural obstacles and setbacks, and human life constitutes at best a gradual decline and descent in the direction of death (verses 17–19). This situation is entirely the opposite of that which God had intended for His creation. Pain and suffering are *our fault*, a fault inherited from our forebears.

Thus the questioners in Matthew 9 were partially correct, though Jesus points out that God will bring redemption to humans and eradicate their tears, pain, suffering, and death (Revelation 21:4) once the new heavens and the new earth are ushered in to restore the original state of pristine paradise. This is a living hope to which we can all look forward. Jesus manifested God's glory in restoring the sight of this blind man—a miniscule hint of the final redemption pulled forward. Since all humans have at least initially rejected God, and all have offended Him through their sin, He is under no obligation to save or heal any of us. He may and does choose to do so, however, through His infinite mercy and grace.

On a rational, logical level, this question should not matter one iota to the atheists, since in an atheistic system no allowance is made for absolute morality. In its absense there is ultimately no such thing as good or evil. Everything is relative, implying that what may be deemed bad for one man may well be considered good for another. Atheism presupposes and depends upon naturalistic evolution, red in tooth and claw. Suffering, death, and even mass extinctions, having happened for billions of years, are a completely natural part of atheism, and suffering makes no difference whatsoever. Many atheists support abortion, which is from a moral standpoint nothing less than the murder of an innocent unborn child in the safest of all places, inside its mother's womb. Yet 42% of all deaths today worldwide are the result to medically induced abortions. Many atheists, far from being neutral on the subject of death, positively support it. This is both a stark contrast and a great contradiction, since atheists accuse God many times for senseless murder. At the very least these discrepancies should drive more atheists to become pro-life, if they want to remain consistent humanists who are concerned for the good of humanity.

The question of suffering still lingers. How can theists or Christians respond? By nature I am a melancholy person. Melancholy individuals tend to experience suffering at a deeper level than other people and can easily relate to others' suffering. Yet for all the suffering I myself have endured (for example, my father was psychologically abusive and parted from my family when I was thirteen), I can still assert that there is meaning in pain. It is a means, I think, for God to get through to His creatures, a reminder for us to live more holy lives since we as a race brought the suffering upon ourselves.

Hebrews 5:2–3 notes of Jesus Christ that He "can have compassion on the ignorant, and on them that are out of the way; for that he himself also is compassed with infirmity. And by reason hereof he ought, as for the people, so also for himself, to offer for sins."

It was none other than Jesus Christ, the Son of God, Who took the form of frail humanity and sacrificed Himself upon the cross to vicariously atone for our sins. The sinless for the sinners. The righteous for the unrighteous, to make peace between God and humankind. Jesus' physical death was excrutiating, but it was primarily His spiritual suffering that caused Him anguish: "About the ninth hour Jesus cried with a loud voice, saying, Eli, Eli, lama sabachthani? that is to say, My God, my God, why hast thou forsaken me?" (Matthew 27:46).

Jesus Christ, the second Person of the Trinity, suffered eternal damnation on our behalf on the cross. His was infinite suffering within a finite time frame, something beyond our comprehension. Jesus, though one with the Father, suffered rejection by God, something each of us would have to face had Jesus not borne the consequence in our stead. This is the meaning of salvation, infinitely beyond our comprehension, the ultimate sign of God's love toward us, so wonderful as to leave us in no doubt that God exists, is real, and loves us.

We humans have been experiencing suffering, pain, and death for the 6000 years God's Word tells us this planet has been in existance, ever since the fall into sin. Yet, suffering, pain, and death are all temporary, because God didn't create the world with these realities in mind. One day, we know, all of this will pass away; if we place our trust in Christ we will find ourselves immersed forever in bliss, in eternal happiness without a hint of suffering. God's glorious new earth will last forever, and in eternity all the suffering and pain we have endured will be reduced to a fleeting memory, retreating ever farther behind us as we dwell, fully equipped in our newfound understanding and basking in the presence of a loving and caring God. Isn't this prospect worth our trust in Jesus?

Summary

Suffering is real, a hard and sobering fact of life. Yet God is not indifferent and has a plan to save us from it. Suffering may be meaningless to the atheist, but we who believe cherish the certainty that God sent His Son, Jesus, to die on our behalf to cover our sins, the ultimate source of all suffering. Suffering is transitory, and it will be but a passing memory in Glory.

6

Communism: the first atheist state

The reason I address Communism in this book is that atheists often attack Christians over historical realities like the Crusades or the Inquisition, implying that Christianity cannot be valid because it leads to fanaticism and the wholesale extermination of opposing people groups and religions. [To counter this point, I would call to the reader's attention that the Crusades and the Inquisition were the work of the Roman Catholic Church, which I as a Protestant do not consider to be a part of Christ's true Church. I will discuss this extensively in my future book *Refuting Rome*. Second, I feel the Crusades to have been at least partially justified, since Islamic armies had themselves annihilated large populations of Christians in the Middle East and up until the Middle Ages were attacking France in the West and Hungary in Eastern Europe.]

Atheists frequently claim that the reason there were relatively few nontheists in the Middle Ages is that they were oppressed for such a long time. This might be true, but at the same time it was only with the advent of Darwinism that people found a platform by which they could intellectually adhere to atheism. Let us now examine what atheists are capable of when an atheistic regime such as Communism appears on history's horizon. Since many people in the West were not alive during the rise and zenith of Communism, this opens up a window into that time period during which an all-out attempt was made in certain parts of the world to banish God from the people's collective memory.

The ideology of Communism

Communism—with its distant roots in the secular French Revolution—is an ideology built squarely on evolutionism. Karl Marx, the founder of Communism, dedicated *Das Kapital*, a critique of capitalism, to none other than Charles Darwin. Karl Marx himself was an avowed satanist given to a vile temper, who like Adolph Hitler wanted to exterminate the Jewish people. Communist theory states that the final stage of evolution, following cosmic, chemical, and biological evolution, will be societal evolution, when Communist society will dismantle capitalism and bring about a Utopia where there will be no classes and all people will be equal. Communism is also materialistic, attempting to banish from society any notion of God, substituting the state in a position of supremacy.

The Communists and the Church

A slogan of Marx's Communism included the premises that royalty will rule you, the imperialist army will shoot you, and the Church will fool you. Thus this early brand of Communism made heavy usage of the theory of evolution in its anti-Church propaganda. Belief in God was mocked and ridiculed. Some may point out that people could still go to church during Communism; for a while and to an extent this was true. However, the Church was allowed to perform only acts of charity within society and was banned from proselityzing.

Ultimately the Communists wanted to liquidate the Church, to explunge it permanently from memory. The Church was subjected to spying by secret informants, and in the Soviet Union

Stalin would later blow up buldings of the Orthodox Church. Baptisms had to be performed in secret, and the Church was labeled as reactionary. The Communists wanted to proscribe the topics about which pastors could preach. Anecdotally, a Hungarian pastor was ordered to preach about camels [*tevék* in Hungarian], a seemingly innocuous topic. The authorities instructed him to preach about Acts 7:58 ("And the witnesses laid down their clothes at a young man's feet"—*és lábai elé tevék*).

According to Richard Wurmbrand, the well-known Lutheran pastor who spent 14 years in various Communist prisons in Romania, there were four distinctly different types of pastors. Members of the first type were imprisoned, those representing the second were barely able to stay out of prison, and representatives of the third type to some degree cooperated with the Communists. The fourth type, by far the most evil, was composed of those Judas priests who actively helped the Communists, conspiring against the members of their own churches. Such is the evil nature of the human heart. In the prison system the Communists treated common criminals harshly and right wing inmates even worse. But the pastors received the cruelest treatment of all. Richard Wurmbrand recounts how they slit his throat, starved him in a dark cell for days, and forced him to sign a statement admitting that he was homosexual and that he peed into his open mouth. The guards continuously overheated and then drastically cooled his cell. Upon his release from prison he could hardly recognize himself in the mirror.

Communist torture tools

The methods of torture used during the heyday of Communism were apalling, harking back to the days of the Inquisition. It was as though atheists had learned nothing from those days; once oppressed, they now became the oppressors.

If you visit Andrássy street 60 in the heart of Budapest you can take in an exhibit focused on the methods of torture used during Communism. The torturers would force slender rods of glass up men's penises and then break them, resulting in excrutiating pain for the rest of their lives. Others were obliged to stand upright in a coffin-sized room with lights shining in their eyes and barbs protruding from the walls, reminiscent of the iron maiden from centuries past. Still others were forced to stand in rooms filled with water, with low ceilings only three feet high, forcing the people in the room to get soaked in water. When they came out they could peel off their skin like removing a glove. Hangings were carried out until 1985. The Communists even beat up well-to-do peasants (*kulák* in Hungarian), in line with their principle of not allowing anyone to make undo profits from their livelihood, even though the Communist party was supposed to be that of the workers and farmers.

Communist spies

Approximately 10,000 people were employed as secret service agents in Hungary during the Communist era. The identity of only about 100 was ever revealed, even 20 years after the fall of European Communism. These people reported on the general populace and infiltrated the churches, as mentioned earlier. People became guardedly reserved, fearing to speak openly with one another for fear of divulging confidential issues to someone who might be an informant. They could get into trouble even for trivial infractions like making jokes about Stalin. It was difficult to travel outside the Iron Curtain since many people who did manage to leave never returned. The Communists were paranoid in their belief that people who left the country would either conspire with the imperialist West or introduce unwanted Western ideas or inventions into Communist countries. For example, a Hungarian animal breeder had the chance to meet with the Soviet anti-geneticist Trofim Lysenko, who was inspecting bulls for their fertility. The animal breeder suggested that Lysenko analyze the bull's sperm under the microscope. Lysenko rejected the idea saying that the microscope was an imperialist invention.

Then there was the Hungarian Revolution that started on October 23, 1956. The protest was peaceful in that the people didn't loot stores. However, on that day secret service agents mounted the buildings around Kossuth Square and opened fire upon the people who were demanding basic rights. The Revolution lasted two months, symbolized by young college students throwing molotov cocktails at Soviet tanks that came rolling in after the local authorities proved unable to contain the situation.

Post-Communist Hungary

During the eighteen years I spent in Hungary from my early teens to my early adulthood, I noticed that many people, especially from the older generation, tended to be inordinately reserved. Continuously having to be on the guard against secret informants, they were less talkative than others, especially when it came to religious topics, on which many others were either indifferent or aggressive. Some people were not disposed in the direction of a strong work ethic, assuming that they would always have a job and wouldn't be fired even if they were rude to others, which was the case during Communism. The transition from depending on the government to having to make a living in a competitive environment caused tension and confusion in many people.

Following the demise of Communism the country was in tatters and the state treasury empty. Buildings were crumbling and unsafe. It took up to 20 years to replace the trains and metro cars, covered by graffiti, that had been given to Hungary by the Soviet Union. In neighboring Romania some villages lacked toilets, and some street signs depicted horse-drawn carts instead of automobiles. Half of all Hungarians were without a car, and nobody could procure firearms, which the military and the police hoarded in their efforts to control and coerce the populace. The best firearm one could purchase was an airgun or a gas stun gun, nothing close to what someone might procure at Cabela's or some other modern hunting or outdoor stores in the United States. From the standpoint of someone with experiences like my own, the Second Amendment to the U.S. Constitution is of vital importance.

The former Communist politicans transferred their allegiance to modern political parties, both left- and right-wing. The Hungarian Socialist Party (Magyar Szocialista Párt, MSZP), however, never properly severed its ties to the older Communist Party. This party appealed to Hungarian citizens, and especially to the older generation, by emphasizing security, jobs, and higher wages and pensions, just as the Communist Party had done. However, prices and taxes were also higher. The Socialists promised everything, from free college education to a thirteenth, and sometimes even a fourteenth monthly paycheck over the course of a twelve-month year. Of course, they were at a loss as to where the money was going to come from.

The left wing, as during Communism, tried to keep the people dependent upon the government as the ostensible solution to all their problems. Yet, as history has demonstrated only too well, power corrupts, and absolute power corrupts absolutely. People were given the bare essentials with which to live but were never encouraged to aspire to greater heights of freedom. By this point everybody had a job, a car, a television set, and the basic necessities, but that was all. It was extraordinary to me that the Socialist Party appealed even to people in the churches.

Summary

The Communist system exterminated more than 100 million people in less than a century. It has failed wherever it has ever been tried, be it in the former Soviet Union—despite its vast natural resources— Eastern Europe, Eastern Asia, Cuba, or Latin America. This is the track record of Communism, the first atheist state, and it provides a telling commentary on what atheists are capable of doing once they attain absolute power.

How can we make certain that no atheistic reign of terror will ever again be permitted? Atheists have a lot of explaining to do. Never again.

7

Morality and the appearance of belief in God

Morality

One of the numerous Achilles heels of atheism is that of morality. Many atheists argue in the first place against the existence of God so that they can live their lives the way they want to, without fear of judgment from a supernatural Being Who created them. The basic mentality is "Since God doesn't exist, I can do whatever I want, and nobody will ever catch me." They want to function as their own gods, who both define and run their own lives; some atheists go so far as to openly refer to each individual as a little "god." If God doesn't figure in to life's equation, then according to some evolutionary philosophies humankind represents the pinnacle of the natural world, meaning that we get to make our own rules. Thus some atheists live a life based on the principle of carpe diem, enjoying each day to its fullest and living as though there will be no tomorrow—and certainly no day of reckoning.

It goes without saying that a carpe diem lifestyle can be intensely destructive and immoral. Many atheists, alarmed by this tendency, may be congratulated on opting to live what many would call a decent lifestyle. Based on this trend some atheists have gone on to argue that humans are inherently altruistic, moral in the sense of doing what is good for the community. As true humanists they seek to promote the common good, espousing the model of humans helping humans. They claim that doing good for the community is a positive trait that has developed during the course of human evolution.

However, the idea underlying such altruism suffers from several flaws. Humans are intelligent beings, and some may take advantage of others' industry. If everybody in a community were to become a cheater, total anarchy would ensue, and the human species would rapidly decline. Indeed, some sociological models have shown that cheaters within any given population invariably consist of a minority. Communities tend to balance out, with most people working hard and practicing altruism, but some parasites will always be around.

More importantly, no one person can define what is good for all people. In order to have that ability one would have to solicit the moral opinions of the billions alive on this planet. And we wouldn't be able to ask those who have already passed away—or those who will come in the future, for that matter.

There is no way we as humans could possibly arrive at a moral consensus of what would be good for everyone; only God would be able to do that. Some atheists claim that there exists a moral code apart from God—one to which God Himself should be subjected . . . if He really does exist. However, this code, in order to fit everyone on the planet, would by its nature have to be impossibly complex.

Finally, according to evolutionary theory theistic religions came about in the first place as a form of altruism—based on a desire to do good. This flies in the face, of course, of the basic tenets of Christianity, which stresses the utter destitution of humankind and the race's absolute reliance upon saving grace. The impetus of the faith is not on good deeds but on Christ's righteousness being imputed to undeserving sinners.

A humanistic moral code could at best be relative, and it would have to change as morals and customs did from decade to decade. During the Third Reich the Nazis saw themselves as doing a service to humanity by exterminating Jews. The Communists viewed themselves as bringers of a classless Utopia but ended up precipitating the deaths of more than 120 million people. If morals are relative, what is to prevent another Hitler or Stalin from rearing his head? We should shudder at the mere thought.

If some people view Christian morals as outdated, we will do well to retrain our perspectives by stepping back and being glad we as a human race have made it past Hitler and Stalin. If morals are indeed relative, who are we to say that the twenty-first-century standards for behavior are better than those of medieval times? Will fifty-fourth-century mores be better still? Though human value systems do indeed vary, virtues such as courage, honesty, and diligence are timeless and absolute.

Where did religion come from?

Since atheists believe in evolution, their only response can be that religion, like self-consciousness, must have arisen as a mental faculty of the evolving person, that God is merely a mental construct and not a person, and that belief in God has somehow helped us as humans to better understand our world. This line of reasoning flies in the face of all logic, since it is inconceivable that believing in something false could help anyone move forward in life. Natural selection works only if a positive trait that facilitates individual survival arises within a population.

I cannot help but ask what kind of gene combination could possibly exist to control the individual's worldview? This line of thinking is flatly contradicted by the fact that many people convert to an entirely different system of beliefs, as from atheism to Islam.

Some atheists claim that polytheism, humankind's initial religion, gave way to monotheism, which will ultimately give way to atheism (a decreasing number of gods being the evolutionary trend). Despite a purported modesty, such atheists view themselves as the enlightened pinnacle of humankind. If atheism is truly the summit, I would hasten to contest, how can it explain away the reality that the first atheist state to emerge in history, Communism, is responsible for the deaths of more than 100 million, greatly reducing the size and potential of the human species.

This is not to mention that atheists have killed off other atheists, as was the case when Joseph Stalin orchestrated the murder of his fellow Communist Leon Trotsky, along with other comrades of whom he had become paranoid in anticipation of an attempted power grab (this dynamic was behind the sweeping political purges of the thirties in the Soviet Union).

Contrary to this logic, it would in my mind have made more sense if according to evolutionary theory atheism had been the first religion to arise, followed by monotheism and finally by polytheism—a much more complex paradigm to model a relationship between an individual and a supernatural being, let alone 12 such beings in Greek mythology or 33 billion, as in Hinduism.

However, if God does in fact exist, and has manifested Himself to humankind, as averred in the Judeo-Christian worldview, it would make much more sense if monotheism had come first, since individuals such as Adam, Noah, Moses, Abraham, and the tens of thousands who interacted with Jesus would have claimed to have come into contact with Him. "What advantage then hath the Jew? Or what profit is there of circumcision? Much every way: chiefly, because that unto them were committed the oracles of God" (Romans 3:1–2).

The Jewish people are special in that during a major portion of Old Testament times they were entrusted with the Law, commandments, and knowledge of God. Moses came into physical proximity with God when he recieved from His hand the Ten Commandments. This was an experience that atheists, uncomfortable with the idea of an omnipotent Judge, would want

to expunge from communal memory, using whatever kind of explanation might sound even semi-plausible.

But Christianity is hardly a religion any human being would

have been likely to conceive. People are selfish sinners, and it would not have been to the liking of most to posit a God so holy that He would hold up before humanity a standard nothing short of perfection. Most people would be glad to have a Mr. Always Happy Niceguy for a god—an easygoing, permissive deity who would always bless people, never chastise them, and let them do whatever they wanted.

Yet the Bible makes clear that the situation went so wrong in this world based solely on humanity's fault: pain in childbearing, difficulty at work, physical death—all are aspects of the curse due to our first parents' disobedience toward God. Who could possibly savor with a glad heart the following words from Jeremiah 17:9: "The heart is deceitful above all things, and desperately wicked: who can know it?" Or who of us can avoid the squirm factor when Paul lays it on the line in Romans 3:10, declaring that "there is none righteous, no not one"? These declarations and others like them should crush our egos. The Bible makes abundantly clear— whether or not we appreciate hearing the words or are willing to face their implications—that we are such evil sinners that we need a vicarious external substitute to save us.

During Jesus' earthly life His hard sayings struck some of His disciples as so unpalatable that they opted to turn their backs and no longer walk with Him (John 6:60). Christians are called to take up their crosses daily and sacrifice for others. For example, if someone comes to us in the middle of the night asking for food, we are directed to rise from our beds, open our doors, and give it to them (Luke 11:5–13). If someone hits us on the right cheek we're to turn to them our left as well (Matthew 5:39). Not particularly effective evolutionary defense mechanisms!

If our willingness to accompany someone for one mile (hefting their load for them!) is evolutionarily altruistic enough for the betterment of the human species (Matthew 5:41), what would induce us to voluntarily go that extra mile (surely a waste of energy and resources)? Such counterintuitive thinking baffles evolutionary theory because Jesus' teaching is based not on selfishness or even expediency (motivations basic to evolution) but on self-sacrificing love. The ultimate self-sacrifice of such love was Jesus' willingness to go to the cross to redeem His people from their sins.

Following the resurrection this gospel of self-sacrificing love spread like wildfire throughout the Roman Empire, carried along by the witness of those hundreds of people who had interacted with Jesus and even seen Him after He had risen from the dead. These early Christians sacrificed themselves and even went singing to their deaths at the jaws of hungry lions. They cared for the sick and the outcast—those who according to evolutionary theory would have had weaker genes and should have been left to die off. *This* was real Christianity, unlike the shallow imitation we see so frequently. And everything about it flew in the face of the evolutionary paradigm.

Summary

If Christianity were a product of evolution, the faith's evolutionary success would have to be attributed to characteristics that would, rationally speaking, have caused the movement to disappear from history. According to evolutionary theory, Christianity should never have spread, yet today its presence and power are felt on all inhabited continents. The morality and teachings of the Bible thwart atheistic evolutionary theory. Love triumphs over selfishness.

8

A response to Sam Harris's
Letter to a Christian Nation

Sam Harris's *Letter to a Christian Nation* is a well-known book criticizing American Christianity from an atheistic viewpoint. A National Bestseller, it has been endorsed by the *Wall Street Journal* and a number of leading scientists, including the militant atheist evangelizer Richard Dawkins.

The book is misguided and inaccurate and attempts through flawed exegesis to foist modern concepts onto the Bible. Harris takes up an extremist position and dumps everything negative he can think of about theistic religions onto the reader. Even the title is misleading: America hasn't been a Christian nation for quite some time. It is a highly secularized and liberal country, exporting its lenient philosophy and material excesses to other countries. I would argue that it is impossible for the thinking individual not to see this. Liberalism has spread within the Church to the point that some churches espouse even homosexuality and abortion. Having done door-to-door evangelism and having spoken to dozens of people in the supposedly conservative city of Lincoln,

Nebraska, I can attest to the fact that true, devout Christians are smaller in number than the masses who attend the diluted services of numerous megachurches. Just because someone self-identifies as Christian doesn't make them such. It takes but one look at the Gospel accounts to witness the Jewish leaders arranging for the execution of God's Son!

The false Church is always numerically larger than its true counterpart. Far from being an innocuous, watered down facsimile, the true church is adamantly opposed to the false church. The hypocrites within the institutional Church are many, and it is they who give the Church a bad name. As Jesus makes clear in John 10:27, "My sheep hear my voice, and I know them, and they follow me." A true Christian is a person who hears and then follows Jesus, and that equates to following His commands. Many hypocrites can be referred to as "practical atheists" in that they leave God out of the decision-making equation, acting as though He doesn't exist or, at the very least, isn't important enough for them to factor in. The modern, biblically illiterate Church is a mere shadow compared to that of the book of Acts; of the Reformation; or, more recently, of the Puritans of Holland, England, Scotland, and New England.

Harris's view of the supposed conflict between science (characterized by cold, hard, neutral facts) and worldviews like Christianity (but also atheism) is also misguided, as I have pointed out in previous chapters. Harris also makes the typical mistake of confusing Christianity with Roman Catholicism. Roman Catholicism is basically different from Christianity because of its false gospel of faith and works, falsifying the sacrifice of Christ in the Mass, adding to the Bible, and placing the pope and tradition next to the Scriptures.

Sexuality and abortion

Harris accuses God of genocide and of causing human suffering, yet like many atheists he supports abortion and chastizes the Roman Catholic Church for prohibiting the distribution of contraceptives among AIDS-ridden Africans. Catholic teaching insists that *all* sexual intercourse for reasons beyond procreation is sin. In support of this, they cite the example of Onan in Genesis 38:7-10. Here a man named Judah has three sons, Er, Onan, and Shelah. Er married a woman called Tamar, but was wicked, therefore God killed him. According to Deuteronomy 25:5, in such an event the brother of the deceased man must then marry the deceased man's wife. This is what is happening in verse eight. However, Onan sinned not in that he spilled his seed onto the ground, but because he disobeyed God in having children with Tamar, and thereby being fruitful and multiplying (see Genesis 1:28). Also, according to Paul in 1 Corinthians 7:4-5, "The wife hath not power of her own body, but the husband: and likewise also the husband hath not power of his own body, but the wife. Defraud ye not one the other, except it be with consent for a time, that ye may give yourselves to fasting and prayer; and come together again, that Satan tempt you not for your incontinency."

Whereas the Bible refutes Roman Catholic teaching, we must also guard against sexual promiscuity and immorality. Instead of allowing people, including singles, to give themselves over to sexual promiscuity, we as Christians need to teach them the virtue of self-control in the area of sexual intimacy. If people would practice chastity STDs wouldn't be so widespread.

The section of Harris's book on contraception and abortion contains a couple of sentences that are worth quoting, if for no other reason than their poignant humor: "If you are concerned about suffering in this universe, killing a fly should present you with greater moral difficulties than killing a human blastocyst."

Or consider this gem: "Every time you scratch your nose, you have committed a holocaust of potential human beings. This is a

fact." Ludicrous, since all of those nose cells represent one single individual, having the same genome as opposed to different ones.

Harris disputes the hypothesis of life starting at conception, citing examples of embryos splitting in two or fusing to form a chimera. He asks what happens to the soul(s) of these embryos.

Although God has not seen fit to share this detail with us in His Word, we may be assured that if He endows every human with a soul at the beginning of life, He is certainly free to retake or recycle one of the souls of an embryo that has fused with another. One way or another, we can assume these souls are safe within a benevolent God's safekeeping.

Harris's views on stem cell research are equally mind-boggling. He attacks the dilettante North Korean leader Kim Il Sung's extravagance for filling his duvets with feathers from the chins of seven hundred thousand sparrows, yet insists upon the efficacy of sacrificing human embryos for stem cell research. Modern science is now capable of dedifferentiating somatic cells to make them pluripotent cells. Furthermore, adult stem cells have been used to reproduce whole tissues. For example, cartilage, muscles, and fatty tissues have been regrown from liposuctioned fat, and umbilical cord blood stem cells have been used to generate a liver. Bone marrow stem cells have also been used to regrow a windpipe.

Harris's advocacy of embryonic stem cell research is in my considered opinion inexcusable, especially coming from him as a neuroscientist.

Communist dictators and Hitler

Harris attempts to deflect Christian criticism of dictators such as Joseph Stalin, Kim Il Sung, Pol Pot, and Mao Zedong, all of whom were atheists who opposed organized religion. He refers to them as profoundly idiosyncratic men who were not champions of reason. By this he means that logic and reason, supposedly a hallmark of atheism would never lead people to become such butchers as these men.

Yet these Communists built their countries on atheistic principles. For those of their ilk, human lives have little intrinsic worth, a view diametrically opposed to that of creationists, who insist that humans are fashioned in the image of God and therefore have inestimable value. For atheists such as these, humans are no more than reorganized matter, . . . to them, turning matter into other forms of matter simply doesn't matter.

These individuals desired to liquidate the Church because they thought it wanted to fool people; as we know, religion according to Marx constituted the opiate of the masses, and he considered the Church subversive to society. Soviet citizen Yuri Gagarin, the first man ever to be launched into space, exclaimed that once he was above the Earth he couldn't see God, upon which he based an assumption of His nonexistence. Communist ideology stems from atheistic evolutionary theory, and it was precisely these men's atheism that prompted them to oppress Christianity.

Harris also reiterates an oft-repeated claim that Hitler was Christian. Hitler, in fact, would have nothing to do with Christianity; he was at best nominally Roman Catholic. Some Protestant churches in Nazi Germany may have supported this radical dictator, but these churches were liberal, denying core tenets of the Christian religion (creation, the virgin birth, the resurrection, and most classes of miracles). Albert Speer, Hitler's architect, writes in his memoirs that Hitler tiraded against the Roman Catholic Church and sent ministers, including Martin Niemöller, to concentration camps for preaching against him. Hitler was opposed by evangelical Christians like Dietrich Bonhoeffer and nominally espoused Christianity only because of its supposed usefulness, ultimately rejecting it because it emphasized mercy and grace, not strength and power, the qualities Hitler was looking for in the Arian Übermensch.

In fact, Speer writes that Hitler viewed Islam as a positive religion based on its warlike proclivities, conquering nation after nation as it did during its early days—a pattern Hitler would repeat during World War II throughout most of Europe. To quote from Speer's memoirs, "You see, it's been our misfortune to have the wrong religion. Why didn't we have the religion of the Japanese, who regard sacrifice for the Fatherland as the highest good? The Mohammedan religion too would have been much more compatible to us than Christianity. Why did it have to be Christianity with its meekness and flabbiness?"

Hitler and the Nazis endorsed a version of false Christianity known as Positive Christianity. This worldview rejected 80% of the biblical canon and replaced the Ten Commandments with their own Twelve Commandments. It also emphasized right works instead of right teaching and salvation by grace. Most importantly, it denied that Jesus was Jewish because the Nazis deemed the Jews to be *untermensch*—fit for extermination. The real agenda of German Nazism was the spread of the Arian race, the Übermensch which had its roots in paganism. This was also motivated by the humiliating defeat of Germany at the end of World War I. Nazism was all about the personal cult of Adolph Hitler—and nothing about following Christ.

Well-being

Harris cites statistics indicating that Western countries such as Holland, the Scandinavian countries, Australia, Switzerland, Belgium, and the UK are among the least religious in the world and yet the healthiest. The implication is that atheists are healthier and happier, yet the cold, hard fact is that 11% of adult Danes take anti-depressants. If Danish people were so happy with their lives, then taking anti-depressants should be unheard of amongts them.

Other of Harris's claims are rather stunning. He cites that the ratio of salaries of top-tier CEOs to the average salary in the United States is 475:1. Sobering in itself, but he goes on through some convoluted mental gymnastics to connect this to another statistic, that of 80% of Americans believing in the Judgment Day. *Come again!* We are tempted to challenge. Anyone with a knowledge of statistics knows that virtually any kind of correlation can be made between two completely unrelated phenomena.

Harris also draws a connection between the fact that the American educational system is failing and the statistic that around 50% of Americans deny evolution. To begin with, the shortfalls of the American school system began in my opinion when God was taken out of the schools. Many students whose families also attend church are home-schooled, and home-schooled children consistently outperform students in the often drug- and violence-ridden public schools. This comparison strikes me as an anticorrelation; if anything, it is atheistic secular education that is dumbing down America's students.

Harris tries to delegitimize Christianity with the suggestion that its spiritual experiences are no different from those of other religions, in which people pray, for example, to Allah or Buddha. Besides making a factual error in that Buddha didn't consider himself to be a god, rejecting as he did the many billion gods of Hinduism. It is less widely known that many Muslims convert to Christianity because they consider their prayer lives to be ineffective until they pray to the God of the Bible, who hears and answers them.

The Bible and science

Harris attacks the scientific basis of the Bible, accusing it of conferring an incorrect value on pi. He refers to 1 Kings 7:23–24: "And he made a molten sea, *ten cubits from the one brim to the other*: it was round all about, and its height was five cubits: and *a line of thirty cubits did compass it round about*. And *under the brim of it* round about there were knops compassing it, ten in a cubit, compassing the sea round about: the knops were cast in two rows, when it was cast" (emphasis added). Harris infers that if the diameter of this circle is 10 cubits, and the circumference is 30 cubits, then pi must equal 3. This is incorrect, since he assumes that the basin being described is made up of a shell with a zero thickness. Obviously, since the rim has some thickness to it, it is the *inner* circumference which is 30 cubits in length as mentioned in the passage (meaning a diameter of slightly less than ten cubits), whereas the *outer* diameter must be exactly 10 cubits (with an outer circumference of 10 x pi).

Harris wants to put evolution on an equal footing with the law of gravity because it makes predictions that can be tested. This is true in itself, but what makes a theory a law is that it is observable and repeatable. Evolution is not, at least not in the macroevolutionary sense. Nobody has ever observed a fish transforming into a frog.

Harris himself admits that whatever force jump-started the process of evolution is a mystery. He claims that the basic shape and character of the evolutionary tree of life are well known, yet we must ask what would constitute satisfactory evidence of this, even if we were able to map the evolutionary relationships among all 8.3 million species on Earth—despite the complicating factor that the taxonomies of different groups of species (such as fungi) are always changing.

Interestingly, Harris cites redundancy and regressions as confirmation for evolution. Redundancies are good in themselves; genomes tend to lose genetic material through deletions over time, making it useful to have redundant elements in the genome—spare tires, as it were, in case a gene gets deleted. This also allows for flexibility and easy adaptations between environments. The flightless birds; snakes with pelvises (think back to God's cursing of the snake in Genesis 3:14, obligating it to slide along on its stomach); and fish, salamanders, and crustaceans with nonfunctional eyes, all of which Harris cites, in reality constitute evidence for genetic devolution, not evolution! These anomalies, along with disease-causing viruses, reinforce the point that the world is no longer good, as God created it, but rather under the curse, negatively affected by disease, dysfunction, illness, and death.

Harris also cites vestigial organs, such as gill sacs and tails in humans, supposedly left over from previous epochs of evolution. Yet more than one hundred such vestigial organs have in fact been assigned a function based on further scientific examination.

Harris misrepresents the creation science model, depicting it as insisting that God created all species precisely as they appear today; in reality the creation model deals with variation within animal groups, as stated explicitly multiple times in Genesis 1. For example, Genesis 1:24 says "And God said, Let the earth bring forth the living creature *after his kind*, cattle, and creeping thing, and beast of the earth *after his kind*: and it was so". The Bible does not use our modern concepts of taxonomy. Here the Biblical taxonomical unit is the kind, which corresponds roughly to the taxonomical unit of genus to order. Examples of kinds are the cat kind, the dog kind, the horse kind, or the finch kind, including species such as Darwin's finches. Speciation, or formation of new species can happen within a kind and has been observed.

The Bible isn't antiscientific, as Harris surmises; to the contrary, it mandates science by the very fact that humankind is directed to rule over the creation. Adam was the first taxonomist, and there are at least 130 distinct plant species mentioned in the Bible. 1Kings 4:29-33 mentions the wisdom of King Solomon regarding plant, such as different kinds of trees and animal life, such as beasts, fowl, and fish. This is what Jesus might have been referring to in Luke 12:27 when he mentions that the lilies were arrayed in more glory than him. Psalm 8:8 speaks about the "paths of the sea," which may correspond to underwater pathways such as the Gulf Stream. It is extraordinary that the psalmist, living thousands of years ago in a virtually landlocked environment and lacking any submarine technology, could have had knowledge of such things. Furthermore, contrary to some charismatic ideas Christians may indeed feel free to use medical technology, since God gave us medicine as a natural means for advancing health and well-being. I firmly believe this as someone employed at a medical research university.

A number of hygiene laws are included in the books of Leviticus, Numbers, and Deuteronomy, some of which deal with properly isolating people after coming into contact with dead bodies, contagious skin conditions, and the like (Leviticus 5:2–3, 7:19–21, 11:25–27, 13:1–3, 14:1–8, 15:1–3, 22:4–8; Numbers 9:6-10, 19:1–22, 31:19–20; Deuteronomy 21:22–23, 23:10–11). Other laws describe how to handle or dispose of furniture that has become infected with mildew (Lev. 13:47-59, 14:34-48). The kosher animals mentioned in the Old Testament were mainly herbivores, since carnivorous animals could more likely have been infected with parasites. It is clear that the biblical laws covering kosher animals helped the Jews avoid such diseases.

Religious factioning

Harris also mentions ways in which adherents of various religions demonize members of other religions; he mentions several countries, including Sudan, Nigeria, Ethiopia, Ivory Coast, and the Phillipines, in which Christians and Muslims war against each other. It would be more accurate to state that in Sudan, Ethiopia, and Nigeria Muslims are trying to take over areas that were once Christian; this is what happened in the seventh and eighth centuries, following the advent of Islam.

A doctor friend of mine from South Africa told me about ten years ago that militant Islamic terrorists in South Africa were letting loose their vicious dogs on Christians in the area, and Christians in Ethiopia and Sudan continuoustly fear oppression from militant Muslims. Recently in the news we have heard about Boko Haram, the Islamic terrorist group that took more than 100 Christian schoolgirls captive and forced them to convert to Islam. The plight of Christians in Syria is equally dreadful, with news of beheadings emerging from that region.

Despite the Crusades, which some would view as having been partially justified as attempts to put an end to Islamic violence against Christians in the Middle East, Islamic armies attacked both Western Europe in the eighth century and Southeastern Europe from the fourteenth through the seventeenth centuries. At least three centuries in the history of Hungary were taken up with the continuous struggle between that nation and the Ottoman Empire, which was finally repulsed in 1683 from Vienna (this is why a small portion of Turkey extends into Europe today).

Nevertheless, it cannot be denied that the spirit of the Inquisition and the Crusades is completely contrary to that of Christianity. Allow me to cite Luke 9:51–56 as reinforcement: "And it came to pass, when the time was come that he should be received up, he stedfastly set his face to go to Jerusalem, And sent messengers before his face: and they went, and entered into a village of the Samaritans, to make ready for him. And they did not receive him, because his face was as though he would go to Jerusalem. And when his disciples James and John saw this, they said, *Lord, wilt thou that we command fire to come down from heaven, and consume them*, even as Elias did? But he turned, and rebuked them, and said, *Ye know not what manner of spirit ye are of. For the Son of man is not come to destroy men's lives, but to save them*" (emphasis added).

Conclusion

Harris hopes for "the eradication of religion in our time" and is disappointed that the prospects for this are poor. This is reminiscent of the Communist demonization of theistic religion and its attempts to liquidate the Church. It is unsettling that Harris espouses such dangerous ideas in several books, all of which have been widely distributed. Already people like Bill Nye, the popularizer of certain forms of science, espouse the concept of incarcerating people who deviate from the climate change consensus.

Harris's extremism does not bode well for liberal Christianity, which serves the whims of secularists such as Harris like a faithful lackey. This is because Harris even rejects moderate liberalism, in that he suggests that the reason liberals are moderate is that to be moderate is to believe less and less of the Bible. Liberals cannot have their cake and eat it as well. Liberalism is nonsense; in 1 John 5:13 John tells believers that "these things have I written unto you that believe on the name of the Son of God; *that ye may know that ye have eternal life*, and that ye may believe on the name of the Son of God" (emphasis added).

Harris depicts the God of the Bible as an extremist who coerces people to fear hell, despise nonbelievers, and persecute homosexuals. Paul enjoins believers as follows: "As we have therefore opportunity, let us do good unto all men, especially unto them who are of the household of faith" (Galatians 6:10). We are, in familiar parlance, to love the sinner yet hate the sin. It is rather the self-styled homosexual maffia which is now persecuting Christians, as in the case of how the homosexual movement tried to destroy an Orthodox Presbyterian Church pastor in San Francisco during the eighties.

Harris makes the wild claim that all Christians are extremists who believe in and look forward to our Lord's return when even the elements shall burn with fervent heat (2Pt. 3:10). According to Harris this is just pure violence. Ironically, Harris himself believes in the future heat death of the universe, a sort of naturalistic judgment day, if you will, when all life will face permanent extinction. Judgment Day will involve Jesus Christ judging the living and the dead—without any proactivity on the part of believers. Since we do not know the hour or the day of Christ's return (Matthew 24:36), we should live holier lives instead of becoming more lax.

Conclusion

It is clear that atheism is at best a weakly defensible worldview, guaranteed never to be able to win the argument in the theism-atheism debate. It is basically nothing more than a categorical denial of theism, and as such it brings no intrinsic value to the table. If one is a consistent skeptic one denies all knowledge; this is the very nature of skepticism. In order to be consistent atheism must measure up to the principles of critical skepticism, as one of its leading proponents correctly states.

If we consider that only approximately 0.15% of scientists in the United States are creationists, creation theory can deliver a withering critique of evolution, since belief in God is objective, as opposed to the mere speculation of subjective human beings who weren't there in the beginning to observe how the universe originated. Atheists are correct in positing that natural science does a great deal in the direction of connecting worldview to reality; however, many natural phenomena flatly contradict evolutionary theory, and the creation model explains much more than do the contradictory theories of evolutionary gradualism and punctuated equilibrium.

The creation species model is not only viable and testable but also has a statistical-methodological model to back it up. Other phenomena, such as theophanies and spiritual manifestations, support the existence of the supernatural. Suffering doesn't logically disprove the existence of God either and should not even be an issue for atheists.

Many atheists support abortion and as such are wildly inconsistent with their otherwise humanistic sensibilities. As we have seen, the first atheist state ended up annihilating more than 100 million victims within less than a hundred years. Atheism is one of the most failed worldviews ever, and it behooves us to pose the question *If such an ungodly atheist state were to re-emerge sometime in the future, who is to guarantee that many more millions of lives wouldn't be sacrificed?* Atheism has no absolute morality, precisely because it lives with consensuses and denies all absolutes.

With this, the worldview of atheism has been unraveled, and the tide has turned!

„For the invisible things of him from the creation of the world are clearly seen, being understood by the things that are made, [even] his eternal power and Godhead; so that they are without excuse." (Romans 1:20)

References

All Bible verses were taken from the King James Version.

Science, knowledge and skepticism

- Descartes, R. (1637). Discourse on the Method. Leiden. The Netherlands.

- Keller, T. (2008). The Reason for God. Belief in an Age of Skepticism. New York. Dutton.

- Sagan, C. (1996). The Demon-Haunted World: Science as a Candle in the Dark. New York. Random House Publishing Group.

Proofs for God from creation

- Arrigo, N., and M. S. Barker. „Rarely successful polyploids and their legacy in plant genomes." Current Opinions in Plant Biology 15(2):140–146, 2012; doi: 10.1016/j.pbi.2012.03.010.

- Cserhati, M. (2002). The idea of natural selection from the eighteenth century until today. Budapest. ELTE-TTK Department of natural philosophy.

- —— (2007). „Creation aspects of conserved non-coding sequences." J Creation 21(2):101-108.

- http://www.dissentfromdarwin.org/.

- Colbourne, J. K., M. E. Pfrender, D. Gilbert, et al. (2011). „The ecoresponsive genome of Daphnia pulex." Science 331(6017):555-561.

- Hayakawa S., Y. Takaku, J. S. Hwang, T. Horiguchi, H. Suga, et al. (2015). „Function and evolutionary origin of unicellular camera-type eye structure." PLoS One 10(3):e0118415.

- Ivanyi, S. (2006). Sárkányok születése (The birth of dragons). Szeged, Hungary. Bába Publishers.

- O'Micks, J. (2015). „Bacterial genome decay from a baraminological viewpoint." J Creation 29(2):122-130.

- —— (2015). „Cnidarians turn evolutionary theory into jelly." J Creation 29(3):71-79.

- —— (2016). „Pseudogenes and bacterial genome decay." J Creation 30(1):1-5-III.

- Orengo, C. A., and J. M. Thornton. „Protein families and their evolution—a structural perspective." Annu Rev Biochem 74:867–900, 2005.

- Ouzounis, C. A., V. Kunin, N. Darzentas, and L. A. Goldovsky. „A minimal estimate for the gene content of the last universal common ancestor—exobiology from a terrestrial perspective." Res. Microbiol. 157(1):57–68, 2006.

- Smith, J. M., and E. Szathmary. (1995). The Major Transitions in Evolution. Oxford. Oxford University Press.

- Wood, T. C., K. P. Wise, and M. J. Murray (2003). Understanding the Pattern of Life. Broadman & Holman Publishers. Nashville, Tennesse.

Theophanies and spiritual mainfestations

- MacArthur, J. (1992). Charismatic Chaos. Zondervan Publishing House. Grand Rapids, Michigan.
- ——— (2013). Strange Fire—The Danger of Offending the Holy Spirit with Counterfit Worship. Thomas Nelson, Inc. Nashville, Tennessee.
- White, J. R. (2013). What Every Christian Needs to Know About the Qur'an. Baker Publishing Group. Grand Rapids.

Why is there suffering?

- Cserhati, M. (2015). Franciscan High School. Omaha. CreateSpace.
- Keller, T. (2008). The Reason for God. Belief in an Age of Skepticism. New York. Dutton.

Communism - the first atheist state

- Viktor, O. (2006). 20 years. Heti Válasz Publishers.
- White, J. R. (1996). The Roman Catholic Controversy. Baker Publishing Group. Grand Rapids.
- Wurmbrand, R. (1967). Tortured for Christ. Bartlesville, Oklahoma. Living Sacrifice Book Company.

Morality and the appearance of belief in God

- Jong, J., J. Halberstadt, and M. Bluemke (2012). „Foxhole atheism, revisited: The effects of mortality salience on explicit and implicit religious belief." J. Exp. Social Psychology. 48:983-989.

- http://www.express.co.uk/news/uk/611231/Richard-Dawkins-in-extraordinary-blast-at-Muslims-To-hell-with-their-culture.

A response to Sam Harris's "Letter to a Christian Nation"

- http://creation.com/embryo-design.
- Cserhati, M. (2015). Franciscan High School. Omaha. CreateSpace.
- White, J. R. (1996). The Roman Catholic Controversy. Baker Publishing Group.
- Holding, J. P. (2013). „Was Hitler a Christian?" J Creation 28(1): 35-38.
- https://en.wikipedia.org/wiki/List_of_plants_in_the_Bible.
- McIlhenny, C., D. McIlhenny, and F. York (1993). When the Wicked Seize a City. Huntington House Publishers.
- http://www.merf.org/index.php/fields/africa/.
- Sarfati, J. (2001). Stem Cells and Genesis. http://creation.com/stem-cells-and-genesis.
- Schlafly, P., and G. Neumayr (2012). No Higher Power—Obama's War on Religious Freedom. Washington, DC.

Regnery Publishing, Inc.

- Shortt, B. N. (2004). The Harsh Truth about Public Schools. Chalcedon Foundation.

- Speer, A. (1970). Inside the Third Reich. New York. Simon & Schuster.

- http://www.washingtontimes.com/news/2016/apr/14/bill-nye-open-criminal-charges-jail-time-climate-c/.

- Richardson, C. C. (1995). Early Christian Fathers. New York. Macmillan Publishing Company.

Conclusion

- Witham, L. (1997). „Many scientists see God's hand in evolution." Reports of the National Center for Science Education. 17(6):33.

Acknowledgements

I dedicate this work to the glory of Almighty God, the Creator and Judge Who gave His Son for us. I also hereby acknowledge the help from my mother in proofreading this book as well as all the encouragements that my friends at church gave me in writing this book.

Soli Deo Gloria